THE AMERICAN SUBMARINE

The Nautical & Aviation Publishing Company of America
Annapolis, Maryland

The American

NORMAN POLMAR

SUBMARINE

Title page: The USS *Barb* (SSN-596), photographed off Hong Kong. (Giorgio Arra)

Published in the United States by Nautical and Aviation Publishing Company of America 8 Randall Street, Annapolis, Maryland 21401

Library of Congress Catalog Card Number: 80-85149
ISBN: 0-933852-38X
Printed in the United States of America

The American Submarine was designed by Daniel Kunkel of Cyclone Graphics, Annapolis, Maryland.

Second Edition published in January 1983.

Library of Congress Cataloging in Publication Data

Polmar, Norman.
  The American submarine.

  Bibliography: p.
  Includes index.
  1. Submarine boats—United States—History.
I. Title.
V858.P59   359.813   80-85149
ISBN 0-933852-38X   AACR2

For Rhoda, with affection.

The USS *Grayback* (SS-574); built
as a Regulus missile submarine and
shown here in her current configuration as a commando/frogman transport submarine. (Giorgio Arra)

CONTENTS

Out of her element: The USS *Philadelphia* (SSN-690) sits high and dry in the floating dry dock *Shippingport* (ARDM-4). (U.S. Navy, Jean Russell)

PREFACE

The continued development in U.S. submarine programs has resulted in this second edition of *The American Submarine* being produced just one year after the book was initially published.

After extensive delays the Trident strategic missile submarine has gone to sea. With a submerged displacement of 18,700 tons, the USS *Ohio* (SSBN-726), the first of the series, is the largest submarine yet constructed in the West. The decision was made by Secretary of the Navy John Lehman to deploy the D-5 Trident ballistic missile in these submarines, giving them a striking range of some 6,000 nautical miles with multiple nuclear warheads. This missile will go to sea in 1989 and possibly sooner.

The U.S. Navy's attack submarine forces continues to improve in capability with the delivery of additional units of the *Los Angeles* (SSN-688) class. The increasing Soviet and Third World naval capabilities also have led Secretary Lehman to gain approval of the Defense Department of increasing the number of SSNs from 90 to 100.

Also, the firepower of the *Los Angeles* submarines is being increased by the installation of 12 vertical-launch tubes for the Tomahawk cruise missile. This weapon can be configured for the anti-ship role, carrying a 1,000-pound warhead over 300 nautical miles, or in the land attack role, delivering conventional or nuclear warheads to targets approximately 2,000 nautical miles away. These missiles are in addition to the submarine's four torpedo tubes and score or more of torpedoes, SUBROC missiles, and Harpoon missiles.

In the near-term this 1981 change to the submarine force level was made by converting several outdated Polaris strategic missile submarines to attack boats, mainly by removing their ballistic missile capability. Although these former SSBNs have limited weapons and sensors, and a higher noise level when compared to modern attack submarines, they have none-the-less increased the number of attack submarines available.

However, Secretary Lehman has rejected efforts to reintroduce diesel-electric submarines in the U.S. Navy. When this book went to press five conventional attack submarines remained in U.S. service—the three *Barbels* (SS-580 class), the *Darter* (SS-576), and the *Grayback* (SS-574), the last a commando transport submarine. The German HDW shipyard, the largest builder of diesel submarines in the West during the last 35 years, proposed an advanced, 2,000-ton submarine that would carry the same weapons as a modern SSN, for a fraction of the cost and significantly less manning requirements. Of course, the submarine would be speed-endurance limited. The need for training services from submarines, the value of a diesel submarine's high maneuverability and extremely low noise level, and the ability to base them at the tenders and repairs ships the U.S. Navy normally maintains at Holy Loch, Scotland, in the Mediterranean, and in the Western Pacific have led several members of Congress as well as some naval officers and a number of defense analysts to strongly support the construction of modern diesel submarines for the U.S. Navy. These would be built in American shipyards, with HDW offering the most advanced design available.

* * *

The American Submarine seeks to provide an overview of submarine development and operations in the U.S. Navy. The United States

TABLE 1. SUBMARINE STRENGTH, JANUARY 1983

Type	Active	Under Constn.[1]	Reserve	Class	
Strategic Missile	—	—	2	SSBN–598	*George Washington*
	31	—	—	SSBN–616	*Lafayette*
	2	8	—	SSBN–726	*Ohio*
Attack	—	—	1	SSN–571	*Nautilus*
	1	—	—	SS–574	*Grayback*
	1	—	—	SSN–575	*Seawolf*
	1	—	—	SS–576	*Darter*
	4	—	—	SSN–578	*Skate*
	3	—	—	SS–580	*Barbel*
	5	—	—	SSN–585	*Skipjack*
	—	—	1	SSN–586	*Triton*
	—	—	1	SSN–587	*Halibut*
	1	—	—	SSN–597	*Tullibee*
	13	—	—	SSN–594	*Permit*
	3[2]	—	1[2]	SSN–598	*George Washington*
	5[2]	—	1[2]	SSN–608	*Ethan Allen*
	37	—	—	SSN–637	*Sturgeon*
	1	—	—	SSN–671	*Narwhal*
	1	—	—	SSN–685	*Glenard P. Lipscomb*
	20	19	—	SSN–688	*Los Angeles*
Research	1	—	—	AGSS–555	*Dolphin*
Guided Missile	—	—	1	SSG–577	*Growler*
Total Conventional	6	—	1		
Total Nuclear	123	27	5		
Totals	129	27	7		

Notes: 1. "Under construction" includes submarines authorized through Fiscal Year 1982.
2. Eight older SSBNs have been reclassified as attack submarines; most were operational when this second edition went to press. However, they and the *Skate* SSN as well as the five diesel attack submarines (SS) will be decommissioned during the 1980s.

has made several major contributions to submarine history. The *Turtle* in 1776 made what is believed to be the first attack by a submersible against an enemy ship; the *Hunley* in 1862 was the first submarine to sink a ship in combat; the *Holland* in 1900 was the first submarine formally placed in service by a modern-era navy; the *Nautilus* in 1954 was the world's first nuclear-propelled vessel of any kind; and the *George Washington* in 1960 was the first true strategic missile submarine. Of course, many other American submarines were unique or at least unusual, and at times the United States has boasted the largest submarine fleet afloat.

Today submarines are of major importance in American defense policy, in both their torpedo–cruise-missile attack role and in the strategic nuclear deterrence role. Admittedly, in the 1980s the United States does not possess the largest submarine fleet, the largest individual submarines, or the most innovative undersea craft. All of these superlatives are generally attributed to the Soviet submarine force which in 1982 numbered some 375 active submarines. This was almost three times the number of submarines operated by the U.S. Navy. Still, as indicated in Table 1, the U.S. Navy has a large and highly capable submarine force. However, the very long construction times, high costs, and difficulties in retaining nuclear-trained personnel have created major problems in the American submarine fleet. A decline in numbers of both attack submarines and strategic missile submarines is probable in the 1990s and beyond.

* * *

The author is in debt to many individuals for their assistance in producing this book, especially Mr. Robert Carlisle and his assistant Domingo Cruz; and his former assistant Miss Evelyn Jutte, of the Office of Information, Department of the Navy; Mr. Charles Haberline of the Naval Historical Center; Commander John Alden; and Mr. Paul Silverstone, who kindly provided most of the illustrations. In addition, some of the more recent photographs were taken by my friend and colleague Dr. Giorgio Arra.

NORMAN POLMAR
Alexandria, Virginia

Glossary

AGSS	Auxiliary Submarine	**LPSS**	Amphibious Transport Submarine
APSS	Auxiliary Transport Submarine	**MIRV**	Multiple Independently targeted Re-entry Vehicle
ASSA	Auxiliary Cargo Submarine	**MRV**	Multiple Re-entry Vehicle
ASSO	Auxiliary Oiler Submarine	**NR**	Submersible Research Vehicle (nuclear propulsion)
ASW	Anti-Submarine Warfare		
Crew	designed complement; varies with individual units of the class; generally increases during wartime and during service life of the submarine as more equipment is installed.	**SLBM**	Submarine-Launched Ballistic Missile
		SLCM	Sea-Launched Cruise Missile
		SM	Submarine Minelayer
Displace-ment	surface/submerged displacement (in tons); surface displacement given for earlier submarines.	**Speed**	surface/submerged speed (maximum in knots)
		SS	Submarine
		SSA	Cargo Submarine
Depth	designed operating depth (in feet)	**SSBN**	Fleet Ballistic Missile Submarine (nuclear propulsion)
DSRV	Deep Submergence Rescue Vehicle	**SSG**	Guided Missile Submarine
DSSV	Deep Submergence Search Vehicle	**SSGN**	Guided Missile Submarine (nuclear propulsion)
DSV	Deep Submergence Vehicle	**SSK**	Hunter-Killer Submarine
EB	Electric Boat Company (later division of the General Dynamics Corp.)	**SSM**	Submarine Minelayer
		SSN	Submarine (nuclear propulsion)
Guppy	Greater Underwater Propulsion Project	**SSO**	Submarine Oiler
		SSP	Submarine Transport
HTV	Hull Test Vehicle (formerly NR-2) (nuclear propulsion)	**SSR**	Radar Picket Submarine
		SSRN	Radar Picket Submarine (nuclear propulsion)
IXSS	Miscellaneous Unclassified Submarine (dockside trainer)	**SST**	Target and Training Submarine
Length	length overall (in feet)	**USS**	United States Ship

THE AMERICAN SUBMARINE

1. BEFORE HOLLAND

Since antiquity man has been fascinated by the possibility of navigating underwater. Proposals to use such submersibles for military attacks against an enemy's ships or ports soon followed. But probably the first man to actually use a submersible in combat was an American, David Bushnell.

A Connecticut Yankee, Bushnell succeeded in making gunpowder explode underwater, something the Chinese had learned to do some time before. Then Bushnell built his first submarine as a means to use his underwater explosives against the British warships blockading New York Harbor in 1776. The egg-shaped craft was aptly named the *Turtle*. It was made of wood, floated upright in the water, and was just large enough to carry a one-man crew and a maze of gears to drive the craft forward and underwater. Hand-operated propellers could propel the *Turtle* at about three knots and it carried sufficient air to dive underwater for thirty minutes. A detachable explosive device was designed to be screwed into the hull of an enemy ship and

then exploded after the *Turtle* got clear. Bushnell trained an army sergeant, Ezra Lee, to pilot the craft.

The *Turtle*'s first attempt, against HMS *Eagle,* was foiled by the *Eagle*'s copper-sheathed hull. Although discovered, the *Turtle* escaped unharmed. The gunpowder exploded harmlessly and the *Eagle* moved away. In the War of 1812 Bushnell built another submarine which attacked HMS *Ramillies* at anchor off New London, Connecticut. This time the craft's operator succeeded in boring a hole into the ship's copper sheathing, but the screw broke loose as the explosive was being attached to the ship's hull. The attempt failed, but again the submarine escaped.

Robert Fulton's luck was not much better. An American landscape and portrait painter, Fulton went to England in 1794 and began inventing various things—flax spinning machines, a mill for sawing marble, and a device to make rope. Three years later he moved to France and began work on a sub-

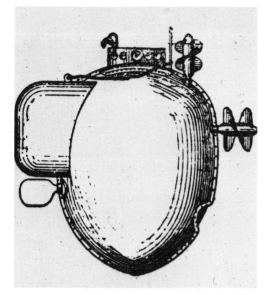

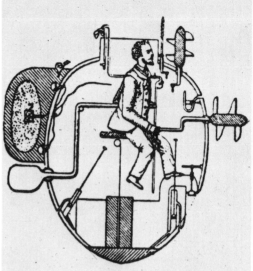

The first American-built submersible was the *Turtle* of David Bushnell. A graduate of Yale University, Bushnell was too frail to operate the complex craft. George Washington commissioned him in the Army's Corps of Engineers, and in his later years he studied and then practiced medicine. These sketches were drawn in 1885 by F.M. Barber from a description left by Bushnell. (U.S. Navy)

These are sketches of one of Robert Fulton's submarine designs—on the surface with sails set, and in its underwater configuration, with masts and spars stowed. Note the small horizontal bow propeller and the stern propeller, the latter disengaged while on the surface. Fulton, who was originally interested in becoming an artist, also designed canals, optical devices—and, of course, steamboats—in addition to submarines. (U.S. Navy)

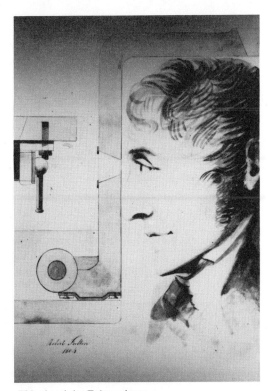

This sketch by Fulton shows a man—probably himself—looking through a Fulton-designed periscope. All mechanical details were provided in his sketches. (U.S. Navy)

marine. Despite successful trials with a model of Fulton's design, the French Minister of Marine would have nothing to do with Fulton's proposal to build a submarine for the French Navy. For the next three years Fulton traveled about Europe, offering his submarine to any government that would listen to his proposals and keeping himself fed by his painting.

In 1800 Fulton returned to France and the new First Consul, Napoleon Bonaparte, gave him a grant to build a submarine. Named the *Nautilus,* the craft was completed in May of 1801. On the surface it was propelled by a sail rigged on a folding mast; when submerged the *Nautilus* was driven by a hand-operated propeller. Built of copper with iron frames, the *Nautilus* submerged by taking water into ballast tanks, and a horizontal rudder—the first use of the diving plane—helped keep the craft steady at the desired depths. The craft contained enough air to keep four men alive and two candles burning underwater for three hours. Later a tank of compressed air was added.

The *Nautilus* was designed to attach an explosive charge to the hull of an enemy ship in much the same manner as the *Turtle.* A test run against an old schooner moored at Brest was successful, with the target being blown to bits. Fulton then set off to attack British warships blockading the the coast of France. But the British men-of-war refused to let the *Nautilus* close on them and although several ships were chased, none were sunk.

Napoleon's interest waned and the Minister of Marine again sent Fulton packing. Disgusted, Fulton crossed the channel and offered his submarine to the British. He gained the ear of Prime Minister William Pitt and was given another chance to test the *Nautilus.* The submarine repeated its Brest performance, this time off Falmer in 1805, sinking the brig *Dorothy.* The demonstration was successful, so much so that, in spite of Pitt's protests, Admiral Lord St. Vincent passed a final judgment: "Pitt was the greatest fool that ever existed to encourage a mode of warfare which those who com-

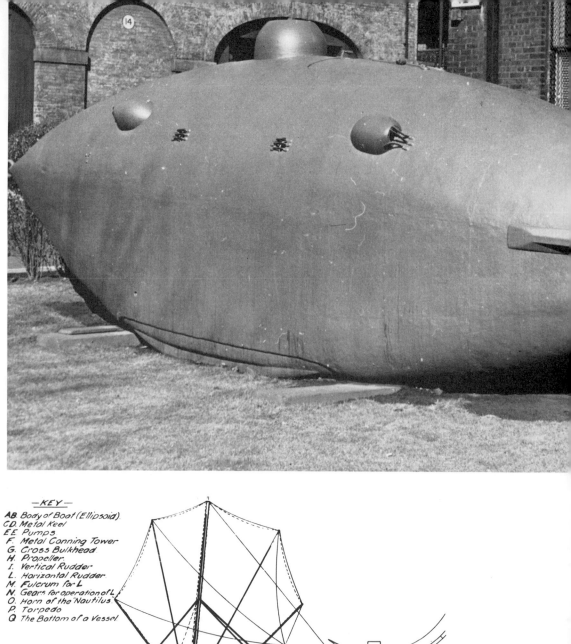

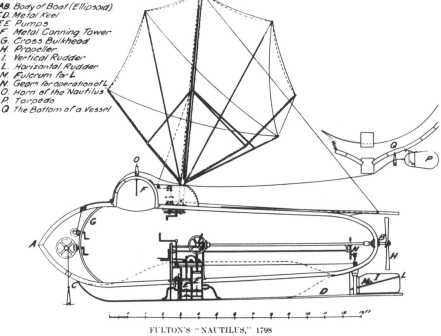

-KEY-
AB. Body of Boat (Ellipsoid).
C.D. Metal Keel
E.E. Pumps
 F. Metal Conning Tower
 G. Cross Bulkhead
 H. Propeller.
 I. Vertical Rudder
 L. Horizontal Rudder.
 M. Fulcrum for L
 N. Gears for operation of L
 O. Horn of the 'Nautilus'.
 P. Torpedo
 Q. The Bottom of a Vessel

FULTON'S "NAUTILUS," 1798

The unsuccessful *Intelligent Whale* at rest at the New York Navy Yard. This was probably the first submarine formally sponsored by the U.S. Government; it was long in construction, and was never really finished. The craft now resides at the Washington Navy Yard. (U.S. Navy)

This cutaway drawing of Fulton's *Nautilus* shows a later and more advanced craft than in the previous sketches. The smaller sketch at right shows how the submarine would use the "horn" (marked O) to attach a "torpedo" (marked P) to the hull of an enemy ship, much the same as did the "weapon system" in Bushnell's *Turtle*. The mast, of course, would be folded down when the craft submerged. (U.S. Navy)

manded the seas did not want, and which, if successful, would at once deprive them of it."

A "failure," Fulton returned to the United States where he persuaded the American Congress to grant him funds to build another underwater boat. This was a more ambitious vessel, capable of carrying one hundred men and driven by a steam engine Fulton himself designed. During the craft's trials, however, Fulton died, and the submarine, named the *Mute,* was forgotten and left to rot at its moorings where it finally sank.

The world's first submarine to sink a ship in combat was the Confederate *Hunley,* which performed this feat toward the end of the United States Civil War. In 1862 Horace L. Hunley of Mobile, Alabama, financed the building of a submarine to help break the Union blockade of the South. Named the *Pioneer,* this craft was 34 feet long and was moved by a hand-cranked propeller operated by three men. It was hoped the *Pioneer* would destroy Union control of the Mississippi River. A letter of marque and reprisal was granted on March 31, 1862, but Union successes forced the Confederates to scuttle the submarine to prevent its capture when Federal forces occupied New Orleans. (Some records say the *Pioneer* was lost with all hands during a dive while en route to an attack on Federal ships.)

The second Confederate submarine was an iron boat intended to be propelled by battery-fed electric motors. But no suitable motor could be found, so a propeller cranked by four men was adopted. The submarine was towed to Fort Morgan at the mouth of Mobile Bay on the Gulf of Mexico. But before it could attack the blockading fleet it sank in heavy seas, without loss of life. This craft was about twenty-five feet long.

The *H.L. Hunley*, the next Confederate vessel, was a modified iron boiler, lengthened to almost forty feet. Water ballast and weights took the boat underwater while eight men inside turned a hand crank connected to a propeller shaft. The craft had a speed of four miles an hour. Its armaments consisted of a torpedo filled with 90 pounds of gunpow-

Water line when ballested to sink

Water line light

This sketch purports to show the Confederate submarine *Hunley* at Charleston, South Carolina, on December 6, 1863. Note the narrow diameter of the craft, in which several men would "lean" side by side to turn the propeller crank. The amidships cross-section shows the position of a crewman when the craft is underway. Although the *Hunley* sank a Union warship, more Confederate sailors died in her than in her victim. (U.S. Navy)

der, towed behind the submarine on a 200-foot line. The *Hunley* was to dive under an enemy ship and surface on the other side, thus dragging the torpedo against the target. After a trial in which the towed torpedo demolished a flatboat, the *Hunley* was moved by railroad to Charleston. There a swell from a passing steamer swamped the submarine, sinking it. Only the commanding officer escaped. The *Hunley* was raised and another crew recruited, but again the craft was swamped. This time the skipper and two crewmen got out. Hunley himself then took command of the submarine and made a successful practice dive. But another dive took Hunley and the entire crew to their deaths. Raised again, the *Hunley* was fitted with an explosive charge fixed to the end of a long spar.

Manned for a fourth time, the *Hunley* made several successful dives. On the night of February 17, 1864, the *Hunley* attacked the Federal warship *Housatonic* off Charleston Harbor. Attacking on the surface at night, the *Hunley* rammed the *Housatonic* with her spar "torpedo." There was a blinding flash of light and a roar that rocked nearby ships and rattled windows ashore. The *Hunley*'s torpedo had exploded the *Housatonic*'s magazine. The explosion sank both ships. All aboard the *Hunley* were lost. Only five men from the *Housatonic* were killed when the steam sloop went down. The *Hunley* had killed about thirty-five Confederate sailors during her violent career. And her one success—the first time an enemy ship is known to have been sunk by a submarine—was accomplished with the undersea craft on the surface during both the approach and the attack.

Some men in the Union were also interested in submarines and in 1864 the Government sponsored the construction of a small, hand-operated metal submarine known as the *Intelligent Whale*. Despite the expenditure of the then-considerable sum of $50,000, the craft was a dismal failure, although the project was not finally abandoned until 1872. This experience would have deterred further submarine develop-

Simon Lake was Holland's principal competitor in the design of early American submarines. (U.S. Navy)

ment in the United States but for the perseverance and genius of John P. Holland and Simon Lake. During the last decade of the 1800s innovative men in many parts of the world were experimenting with submarines, notably Nordenfelt, a Swedish engineer; Bauer, a German mechanic; Laubeuf, a French naval constructor; Holland, an Irishman living in America; and Lake, a brilliant American inventor.

John P. Holland in the conning tower of the USS *Holland* (SS-1). (U.S. Naval Institute)

2. HOLLAND AND LAKE

In light of the foreign interest in undersea craft, in 1888 the United States Government invited bids for a submarine design. The two principal entries in the competition were the Swede, Nordenfelt, and John P. Holland, an ex-Irish school teacher who came to America in 1872.

Holland had launched his first submarine in 1878. This was a 14-foot craft financed by the anti-British Fenian Society, a group that shared Holland's desire to embarrass the oppressors of his Irish homeland. In his concept of underwater warfare, an innocent-looking merchant ship would carry a flotilla of small submarines that could be released in a harbor at night to attack unsuspecting British warships. His second submarine, the *Fenian Ram*, was to be the first of his combat submarines. This 31-foot craft had a 15-horsepower gasoline engine and dived not by being made "heavy," but using diving rudders or planes to submerge, hold depth, and then surface while the submarine retained a small reserve buoyancy. She was armed with

a pneumatic cannon that could fire a six-foot underwater torpedo. For two years Holland tested and modified his second craft, which became a familiar sight on the Hudson River, but it never engaged the British fleet.

Holland won the U.S. Government's 1888 competition to design a submarine and in 1895 he received an order to construct the submarine. The undersea craft, which was named the *Plunger*, was to be propelled by steam on the surface and by electricity when submerged. But Holland believed the Navy's specifications would not produce a satisfactory boat. He was right. After many changes in design the unfinished *Plunger* was abandoned. Holland returned the funds received from the Navy and began construction of another submarine at his own expense.

Launched on May 17, 1897, this Holland craft was powered by a gasoline engine on the surface and battery-fed electric motors while submerged. The Holland boat's armament consisted of a single bow torpedo tube with three torpedoes, and two dynamite

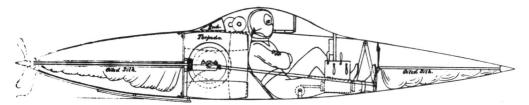

The first U.S. Navy submarine to be officially commissioned into service, the *Holland* (SS-1), in dry dock. Note the steel mask-like covering at the bow for the submarine's dynamite gun. The opening for the *Holland*'s lone torpedo tube is in the center of the bow. (U.S. Navy)

This is a cutaway drawing of Holland's 14-foot submersible. He envisioned several of these craft being launched from innocent-looking merchant ships to attack British warships. The "torpedo" (mine) is immediately behind the operator, who is wearing a diving suit. (U.S. Navy)

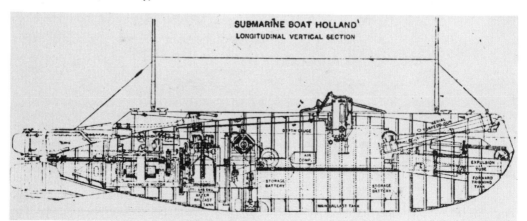

Simon Lake's submarine *Argonaut* under construction in a Baltimore dry dock, about 1898. Lake's interest in submarines began at age ten or eleven when he read Jules Verne's *Twenty Thousand Leagues under the Sea*. His original submarine, *Argonaut Junior*, was a 14-foot, two-man craft with a bottom hatch through which small objects—including fish—could be recovered. (Maryland Historical Society)

The *Moccasin* (SS-5) underway off Suffolk, Long Island, New York, about 1903, with officers seated atop the "turret" and a sailor working on a ventilator. These early submarines were given marine creature names until November 17, 1911, when they were assigned letter-number class names. (U.S. Navy)

guns. The guns, one facing forward and the other aft, were aimed by steering the submarine itself in the direction of the target. The submarine was purchased by the Navy on April 11, 1900, and commissioned the following October 12 as the USS *Holland* (SS-1).

Holland's only significant contemporary in the United States was Simon Lake. Lake's first submarine, the *Argonaut 1*, was privately built in 1894. Lake's boat was similarly powered by a gasoline engine and electric batteries, and was fitted with wheels for rolling along the bottom of the sea. He envisioned divers being sent out from submarines to cut cables, destroy mines, and telephone enemy movements back to a shore base. For underwater cruising the wheels could be retracted into the hull. Lake's important contributions to submarine design included the use of four wing-like diving planes, two forward and two aft, that could keep a submarine at a constant depth, even at slow speeds, without changing the craft's ballast.

In 1898 Lake's *Argonaut* sailed from Norfolk to New York under its own power, becoming the first submarine to navigate extensively in the open sea. Lake's second submarine was the *Protector*, a greatly improved vessel launched in 1901. After the United States rejected the *Protector*, Lake offered it to Russia and Japan. Russia bought it and ordered five more like it. (Japan bought several Holland boats, but neither side used them in the Russo–Japanese conflict of 1904-5.) And the Royal Navy, long opposed to undersea craft, purchased five Holland-type boats to be delivered in 1902, Britain's first submarines.

The U.S. Navy was now firmly committed to submarines. Admiral George Dewey, the hero of the recent Spanish-American War, had told a Congressional committee that if the Spanish had possessed two submarines at Manila, "I never could have held it with the squadron I had." He noted that the submarine "is infinitely superior to mines or torpedoes or anything of the kind . . . With two of those in Galveston [Texas] all of the navies

The USS *Plunger* (SS-2) underway. The officer looking back at the camera is believed to be Lieutenant Charles P. Nelson, her first commanding officer. President Theodore Roosevelt made a dive in the *Plunger* on March 25, 1905. He told of the adventure by declaring, "Never in my life have I had such a diverting day . . . nor so much enjoyment in a few hours." The *Plunger*'s last commanding officer, from 1909 to 1910, was Ensign Chester W. Nimitz. (U.S. Navy)

Simon Lake's *Argonaut* underway on the surface about 1898. The craft had wheels to be used for rolling along the bottom, since Lake intended the *Argonaut* to support divers working on the ocean floor. Although no torpedo tubes were fitted, divers from the submarine could plant mines against warship bottoms. Cuban revolutionaries offered Lake $3 million in gold bonds if he would sell them the craft. (U.S. Navy)

The A-boats *Grampus* (SS-4) and *Pike* (SS-6) under repair at San Francisco. Although designed by John P. Holland, the A-boats were built by the Crescent Shipyard in Elizabeth, New Jersey, and the Union Iron Works in San Francisco. Note their hull shape, somewhat similar to later "tear-drop" submarines, and the minimal superstructure. (U.S. Navy, Paul H. Silverstone)

of the world could not blockade the place."

The Navy then ordered a procession of Holland-designed boats, beginning with the "A" class. Originally assigned names beginning with the *Plunger*, these were enlarged versions of the *Holland*, being 63¾ feet long, displacing 107 tons on the surface, and having a single 18-inch-diameter torpedo tube in the bow. These small boats were intended to defend ports, and in 1909 six of the seven A-boats were sent to the Philippines as deck cargo on Navy colliers to defend Manila against hostile attacks.

Their seven-man crews lived ashore, or aboard whatever ship was available to be designated as a tender. The coastal monitors built in the previous century were popular in this role because of their low freeboard and ample facilities. The A-boat skippers were ensigns, a couple of years out of the Naval Academy, whose submarine training consisted of a few practice dives with their predecessors. (In 1917 the Navy established a formal submarine school at New London, Connecticut.)

Successive Holland designs followed for the U.S. Navy, each slightly larger with improved capabilities. Holland's monopoly on U.S. submarines was questioned by many, as an intense rivalry developed between Holland and Lake. In 1907 the Navy held competitive trials between Holland's *Octopus* (SS-9) and Simon Lake's experimental submarine *Lake*. Following the trials, the Navy concurrently built submarines to the designs of both men. Going further afield, the Navy also built one submarine, the G-4 launched in 1912, to the plans of Italian designer Laurenti, but the craft lacked stability and was unsuccessful. In general, Lake's designs were too complex and the Navy built more Holland-type boats, from 1924 onward at the Electric Boat Company at Groton, Connecticut.

By the time of American entry into World War I in April 1917, the L-class submarines were being built. These were 165-foot, 456-ton submarines with diesel engines for surface propulsion as well as for battery-charging. Diesels were more reliable and

TABLE 2. HOLLAND–LAKE ERA SUBMARINES

Hull Numbers[1]	Number Completed	Class[2]	Launched	Surface Displacement	Length Overall	Speed	Torpedo Tubes
SS–1	1	Holland	1898	64	53¾	8/5	1 18-in.
SS–2 to 8	7	A	1901–1903	107	63¾	8/7	1 18-in.
SS–9 SS–13 to 16	5	C	1906–1909	238	105¼	10½/9	2 18-in.
SS–10 to 12	3	B	1906–1907	145	82½	9/8	2 18-in.
SS–17 to 19	3	D	1909–1910	288	134¾	13/9½	4 18-in.
SS–20[3]	1	G–1	1911	288	134¾	13/10	4 18-in.
SS–20 to 23	4	F	1911–1912	330	142½	13½/11½	4 18-in.
SS–24 to 25	2	E	1911	287	135¼	13½/11½	4 18-in.
SS–26	1	G–4	1912	360	157½	14/9½	4 18-in.
SS–27 SS–31	2	G–2	1912–1913	300	161	14/10	4/6 18-in.[5]
SS–28 to 30 SS–147 to 152	9	H	1913–1918	358	150¼	14/10½	4 18-in.
SS–32 to 39	8	K	1913–1914	392	153½	14/10½	4 18-in.
SS–40 to 43 SS–49 to 51	7	L–1	1915–1916	450	167½	14/10½	4 18-in.
SS–44 to 46 SS–48	4	L–5	1916–1917	456	165	14/10½	4 18-in.
SS–47	1	M	1915	488	196¼	14/10½	4 18-in.
SS–52 SS–60, 61	3	AA[4]	1918–1919	1,107	268¾	20/10½	6 21-in.
SS–53 to 59	7	N	1916–1917	340	147½	13/11	4 18-in.
SS–62 to 71	10	O–1	1917–1918	521	172¼	14/10½	4 18-in.
SS–72 to 77	6	O–11	1917–1918	491	175	14/10½	4 18-in.
SS–78 to 97	20	R–1	1917–1919	530	186¼	13½/10½	4 18-in.
SS–98 to 104	7	R–21	1918–1919	510	175	14/11	4 18-in.

1. The prefix symbol SS was assigned to U.S. Navy submarine hull numbers in 1920.
2. Early U.S. submarines were originally named; they were reassigned letters and numbers in 1911.
3. The number SS–20 was assigned to the G–1 after the loss of the F–1 in 1917; previously the G–1 was designated SS–1
4. These boats were renamed T–1 to 3 in 1920; they were later redesignated SF–1 to 3 for Fleet Submarine.
5. Four tubes in SS-27; two additional deck tubes in SS-31.

The torpedo room of the *Adder* with 18-inch torpedoes ready for loading into the craft's single bow torpedo tube. There were several accidents with these early boats, with the *Pike* (SS-6) being sunk by an explosion (later salvaged), and the *Porpoise* (SS-7) losing all of her crew in an internal explosion. (U.S. Navy)

Guns	Crew	Depth	Design
2 dynamite	7	100	Holland
nil	7	150	Holland
nil	15	200	Holland
nil	10	150	Holland
nil	15	200	Holland
nil	15	200	Lake
nil	22	200	Holland
nil	20	200	Holland
nil	24	200	Laurenti
nil	25	200	Lake
nil	25	200	Holland
nil	28	200	Holland
1 3-in.	28	200	Holland
1 3-in.	28	200	Lake
1 3-in.	28	200	EB
2 3-in.	38	150	EB
nil	25	200	EB
1 3-in.	29	200	EB
1 3-in.	29	200	EB
1 3-in.	29	200	EB
1 3-in.	29	200	EB

considerably safer than the gasoline engines with their volatile gasoline and dangerous fumes. For armament the L-boats had four 18-inch torpedo tubes in the bow and, on the deck, a single 3-inch gun for attacking small surface ships. The 3-inch/23-caliber gun* then in use was housed in a watertight well beneath the deck. It was raised to the firing position by a hydraulic mechanism. When stowed, the barrel was in a vertical position, projecting up through the well, with its circular shield forming the cover for the well. The gun was too small to be effective against any but the lightest enemy craft. The L-boats' speeds were relatively high: 14 knots on the surface with diesels and 10½ knots submerged with electric motors.

When America entered the war there were some fifty submarines in service, ranging from the small A and B boats in the Philippines, to the advanced L boats. (Germany had about twenty small U-boats in service when the war began in 1914.) With American declaration of war against Germany in April 1917, the Navy sent much of the fleet to British waters, beginning with a destroyer division a few days after entry, and then more anti-submarine ships to help protect Allied convoys from marauding U-boats. Later the battleships followed and U.S. submarines were sent to various bases, from the mid-ocean Azores to Queenstown in Ireland. About twenty American submarines reached the war zones but saw little action, as the German surface fleet had already been driven from the high seas. Some of the K and L boats serving in European waters had encounters with U-boats, but no kills were credited to the Americans. Rather, World War I served to demonstrate the tremendous power that submarines could bring to bear, for U-boats almost brought victory to the Germans.

*The caliber is the length of the gun, i.e., the 3-inch inner barrel diameter multiplied by 23, or 69 inches long.

A school of U.S. submarines during World War I: from left, L-3 (SS-42), L-4 (SS-43), L-9 (SS-49), L-10 (SS-50), and L-11 (SS-51). The letter A was added to their markings to distinguish them from the British L-class submarines. Large markings, it was hoped, would quickly identify them to Allied anti-submarine forces. Note the 3-inch guns forward of the conning towers in the stowed position. (U.S. Navy)

The *Argonaut*'s engine room, looking aft. The *Argonaut* is believed to have been the first submarine to operate extensively in the open sea. Both the *Argonaut* and *Plunger* were launched in August 1897. The latter submarine suffered from design problems and never had a fully successful submersion. While the *Argonaut* was a success, she too suffered problems, as did most other early submarines. (U.S. Navy)

The *Holland* was assigned to the U.S. Naval Academy at Annapolis in October 1900, arriving there under tow from Newport, Rhode Island. She remained there as a training craft until 1905, except for a training cruise back to Newport. The submarine was then assigned to Norfolk, Virginia, until stricken on November 21, 1910. Here midshipmen from the Naval Academy Class of 1902 visit the *Holland*. Note the officer, sailor in working clothes, and ship's bell on the near mast. (U.S. Navy)

Submarines under construction in a covered building way at the Portsmouth Navy Yard in July 1918. In the pre-nuclear era, the Portsmouth yard, actually at Kittery, Maine, built more submarines for the U.S. Navy than any other yard. At left is the O-1 (SS-62) and at right, with pressure hull incomplete, the S-3. (SS-107)

Simon Lake's *Protector* at sea. She was larger and more complex than his *Argonaut*, but suffered from a number of difficulties. Note the large conning tower with port holes, two open hatches on the deck and one on the conning tower, and the wheel and compass for surface navigation. (U.S. Navy)

The *Tarpon* (SS-14), one of the C-boats, underway on the surface. Each class of the submarines was larger and more refined; note the rounded bow for both surface and underwater performance. Both periscopes are in the raised position. (U.S. Navy)

The *Seal* (SS-20) backing down slowly, with hatches on her large casement superstructure open, and a torpedo recovery crane fitted foward. This-Lake designed submarine was the first built by the Newport News Shipbuilding and Dry Dock Company in Virginia, today one of only two U.S. yards engaged in submarine construction. (U.S. Navy)

The *Narwhal* (SS-17) at high speed. An awning structure is installed over the conning tower. The D-class boats were the last U.S. submarines with gasoline engines for surface propulsion. The use of diesels in later classes reduced the danger of explosion and fire from highly volatile gasoline. (U.S.Navy)

The G-4 proved to be very unsatisfactory in U.S. service, especially because of her lack of stability. Note the small conning tower and the small stern rudder atop the after hull section.(U.S. Navy)

The big and the small: the *Holland* and the tsarist Russian battleship *Retvizan* enter a dry dock at the New York Navy Yard, probably in 1901, although it might have been as late as 1902. After completion in 1902, the *Retvizan* sailed for the Baltic and was then dispatched to the Far East. After seeing extensive action she was sunk in harbor by Japanese guns, then refloated and placed in service as the Japanese *Hizen*. (U.S. Navy)

The entire class of five C-boats are dwarfed in the Gatun locks of the Panama Canal. All five operated in the Panama area during World War I, intended for the harbor-defense role if German warships should threaten the region. (U.S. Navy)

Two A-boats are loaded aft as deck cargo aboard the collier *Caesar* (AC-16) en route to the Philippines. All of the A-boats except the *Plunger* (SS-2), as well as most of the B and C classes, were based in the Philippines. (U.S. Navy)

The *Holland* underway, "buttoned up" and ready to dive, except that her two folding masts are in the raised position. Note the small "turret"—predecessor to later conning towers—with several thick glass windows. The *Holland* did not have a periscope. According to the description of Holland's chief engineer, the craft "is completely lighted by electricity; has a water-closet; and a crew of six men can comfortable live aboard for forty hours." (U.S. Navy)

A sailor helps load a torpedo aboard the *Adder* (SS-3) at the Cavite Navy Yard in the Philippines about 1912. The "fish" is going in tail first. Cavite was a U.S. submarine base from 1909 until early 1942, when the islands fell to the Japanese assault. (U.S. Navy)

The *Thrasher* (SS-26), designed by Laurenti of Italy, was probably the only U.S. submarine built essentially to a foreign design, although many European features have been incorporated in American submarines. This photo shows the submarine as the G-4 at Philadelphia in October 1912. (U.S. Navy, Paul H. Silverstone)

The *Salmon* (SS-19) submerging, with her twin periscopes leaving a "feather" wake. Note the small "fish" flag, warning that there is a submarine below. Later the symbol was also adopted for submarine rescue ships to indicate that a submarine was in the area. (U.S. Navy)

The crew of the *Adder*, plus a couple of men probably aboard for training, pose for the photographer. Note the superdeck built over the conning tower and the thirteen-star flag. At the time, submarine service earned sailors five dollars a month extra pay. Qualified submariners also received one dollar for each day during which the submarine dived, up to a maximum total of twenty dollars per month in "submarine pay." (Frederick M. Lindley)

The *Haddock* (SS-32) making knots in rough seas. Note the array of radio antennas. There is a torpedo recovery crane rigged forward, an awning over the conning tower, and a sailor standing by the open after hatch. Submarine duty has always been arduous, but especially in the small, cramped boats of pre-World War I construction. (U.S. Navy)

The submarine K-5 (SS-36) in Hampton Roads, Virginia, on December 13, 1916, makes an imposing sight, despite the sailor on deck bending over. The K-5 and three other K-boats served off the Azores during World War I. (U.S. Navy)

The obsolete monitor *Tallahassee* (BM-9, formerly the USS *Florida*) in service at Hampton Roads as a submarine tender on December 10, 1916. The submarines K-5 and K-6 are moored alongside. The monitors were used to provide office space and berthing for the submariners, as well as providing supplies and maintenance support. (U.S. Navy)

The paperwork will be done! A sailor uses a Corona typewriter while sitting on a hydrophone head on the submarine H-5 (SS-148) at San Pedro, California. Note the conning-tower configuration and narrow deck with stanchions fitted; they will be taken down when the submarine puts to sea. (U.S. Navy, J. Edwin Hogg)

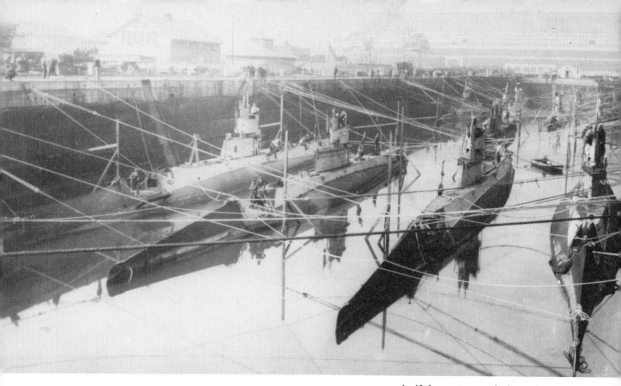

As if they were caught by a giant spider, eleven submarines are moored amidst a web of lines in Drydock No. 2 at the Philadelphia Navy Yard after World War I. After this photo was taken in October 1919 some were scrapped, some cannibalized, and some returned to active service. (U.S. Navy)

A sailor holds the hydrophone sound head aboard the submarine H-5 (SS-148) in San Pedro about 1919. During World War I hydrophones were used to translate underwater sounds into electrical output for transmission to an operator's earphones. This was the start of "passive sonar." (U.S. Navy, J. E. Hogg)

The K-2 (SS-33) at sea in a dazzle camouflage scheme. The design—which extended to the K-2's conning tower and periscope shears—was intended to confuse a German U-boat skipper viewing the sub through a periscope. It is unlikely that any of the camouflaged boats reached the war zone. (U.S. Navy)

Submarine under sail: while searching for a missing tug east of Hawaii, the R-14 (SS-91) lost propulsion. Sheets and canvas were sewed together and, using her periscopes for masts, the submarine was under sail for five days, arriving at Hilo, Hawaii, on May 15, 1921. (U.S. Navy)

Sailors from several O-class submarines nested together assemble on the O-12 (SS-73) in preparation for going ashore on liberty. The wash is hung out on the other submarines. (U.S. Navy)

The first U.S. submarine to be designated as a "fleet" submarine was the *Schley* (SS-52), later designated AA-1 and then T-1. In addition to four bow torpedo tubes, four more were fitted into the superstructure (see dark rectangle just behind the conning tower). The three submarines of this type were unsuccessful, having deficiencies in their hull design, engines, and armament, with their operating depth being only 150 feet. Later a 4-inch gun was mounted forward of the conning tower. (U.S. Navy)

The *Argonaut* (SM-1 and later SS-166 and APS-1) was the largest American submarine built until after World War II. Here she is shown in the 1930s with her forward 6-inch/53-caliber gun being aimed to port. (U.S. Navy)

3. BETWEEN THE WARS

The Great War of 1914-18 graphically demonstrated the effectiveness of submarines in combat. Diminutive German U-boats almost severed sea communications to Great Britain, bringing the nation to the verge of surrender. Only the use of convoys to protect merchant ships, and of American antisubmarine forces reinforcing the limited British ASW resources, made victory over the U-boats possible.

Despite immediate postwar efforts by many groups to ban submarine warfare entirely, most of the world's navies continued to be interested. The S-boats were in many respects the first American postwar submarines. Although begun during World War I, the S-class submarines represented a new approach to submarine development in the U.S. Navy. The previous classes through the R-boats shared some features with the S-class. However, whereas the earlier U.S. submarine classes were each designed and built by a commercial firm after being given specific military characteristics by the Navy,

the S-class was designed and built through a competitive process.

The Electric Boat Company (successor to Holland) was awarded a contract to design and build the S-1,* the S-2 was ordered from the Lake Torpedo Boat Company, and the S-3 was designed by the Navy Department and built at the Portsmouth Navy Yard in Kittery, Maine. The Navy planned to take the best design features of each prototype and combine them into a single class for subsequent mass production.

With the end of World War I in November 1918 the construction pace for the S-boats as well as other U.S. warships slowed. Still,

*The Holland–EB submarines of the S-class were actually built under subcontract at the Fore River Shipbuilding Company (later Bethlehem Steel) in Quincy, Mass., and at the Bethlehem Steel yard in San Francisco, Calif. In 1924, the Electric Boat Company received an order for four submarines from Peru and expanded its diesel-engine plant at Groton, Conn., into a building yard. These Peruvian and all subsequent U.S. submarines built by EB were built at Groton, across the Thames River from New London.

The submarine S-49 (SS-160) in heavy seas with ice on her running lines. The S-boats formed the backbone of the U.S. submarine force during the 1920s and early 1930s. Several saw combat in World War II, with five being transferred to Great Britain and one to the free Polish naval forces. (U.S. Navy)

An electric motor-generator is lifted from the S-44 (SS-155) undergoing repairs at Coco Solo in the Canal Zone in 1926. There is an opening cut in the submarine's superstructure and a "soft patch" has been unbolted from the inner pressure hull. Until World War II, submarines had such patches to facilitate equipment repairs and replacement. Later submarines had welded areas that could be easily opened up. (U.S. Navy)

The Commander, Submarines, U.S. Asiatic Fleet, boards the S-40 (SS-145) for inspection. Note the shape of the outer hull structure to accommodate the 4-inch gun in this 1935 photo. (U.S. Navy)

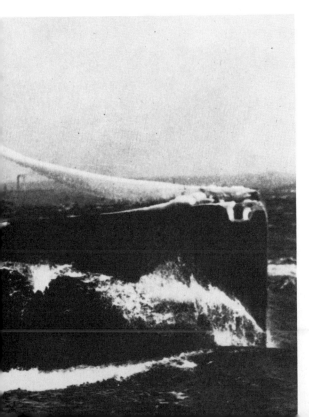

fifty-one of the S-boats were completed through 1925—thirty-one to the Holland-EB design, fifteen to the Navy design (including four built by Lake), and five to Lake designs. The Lake prototype S-2 was not successful and the four later Lake boats, the S-48 through S-51, were of a larger, improved design. Indeed, the size of the S-boats varied considerably, with their surface displacement ranging from 800 tons up to 1,000 tons (see Table 2). Among other features, the S-10 through S-13 were the first U.S. submarines to have a stern torpedo tube.

The S-boats were the mainstay of the Navy's submarine force in the between-war period. But they had numerous problems, and the headline "S-boat Sinks" was frequent in the American press between the wars. The S-5 sank during a test dive off the Delaware Capes in 1920. Flooding through the main air induction valve to the engine spaces resulted in the boat sinking in 194 feet of water. The after ballast tanks were blown dry until the stern of the submarine stuck up 17 feet out of the water. Then, with the help of passing steamers, a hole was cut in the stern and the entire crew escaped. The S-48 sank in 1921, the S-36 and S-39 sank in 1923, all without loss of life. But the S-51 was rammed off Block Island, Rhode Island, by a steamer on the night of September 25, 1925, and only three men survived from the crew of thirty-six.

Two years later, the S-4 was rammed by a Coast Guard destroyer off Provincetown, Massachusetts. The stricken submarine came to rest at a depth of 110 feet. Six men in the forward torpedo room were able to slam and dog the bulkhead door as the submarine started down, sealing themselves off from the three other compartments. The remaining thirty-four men in the submarine were forced to evacuate the next two watertight compartments, the battery room and control room, finally taking refuge in the aftermost compartment consisting of the engine and motor rooms. They had no chance of raising the submarine themselves. Inside the stricken submarine the temperature was two degrees above freezing. On the surface bad

The S-22 (SS-127) shows off her bow lines at the Portsmouth Navy Yard on November 21, 1929. Note the modified escape-hatch chamber forward of the gun, with a torpedo loading chute immediately behind it, and the 4-inch gun swung out to port to clear the loading chute. The S-22 went to Britain in 1942 as HMS P-554. (U.S. Navy)

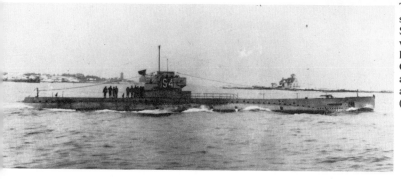

The S-4 (SS-109) shows off the odd-shaped conning tower of the S-boats. She was lost on December 17, 1927, when a Coast Guard destroyer ran her down off Provincetown, Cape Cod. Her entire crew was lost, although six men survived for several days in the forward torpedo room. (U.S. Navy)

TABLE 3. BETWEEN-WAR SUBMARINE CLASSES

Hull Numbers	Number Completed	Class	Launched	Displacement[1]	Length Overall	Speed	Torpedo Tubes[2]	Guns	Crew[3]	Depth
SS–105 SS–123 to 146 }	25	SS–1	1918–1921	800/1062	219½	14½/11	4/0 21-in.	1 4-in.	38	200
SS–106	1	S–2	1919	800/977	207	15/11	4/0 21-in.	1 4-in.	38	200
SS–107 SS–109 to 122 }	15	S–3	1918–1920	875/1088	231	15/11	4/0 21-in.	1 4-in.	38	200
SS–108	—	Neff	Planned submarine using the Neff propulsion concept of employing diesels for both surface and underwater propulsion; not built.							
SS–159 to 162	4	S–48	1921	903/1230	267	14½/11	4/1 21-in.	1 4-in.	38	200
SS–163 to 165	3	Barracuda (V–1)	1924–1925	2000/2620	341½	21/8	4/2 21-in.	1 5-in.[4]	56	200
SS–166 (SM–1)	1	Argonaut (V–4)	1927	2710/4164	381	15/8	4/0 21-in.	2 6-in.	88	300
SS–167 to 168	2	Narwhal (V–5)	1929–1930	2730/3960	371	17/8	4/2 21-in.	2 6-in.	88	300
SS–169	1	Dolphin (V–7)	1932	1560/2215	319	17/8	4/2 21-in.	1 4-in.	57	250
SS–170 to 171	2	Cachalot (V–8)	1933	1110/1650	271 5/6	17/8	4/2 21-in.	1 3-in.	43	250

1. Displacement surfaced/submerged.
2. Bow/stern torpedo tubes; the S–10 to 13 also had one stern torpedo tube.
3. Designed crew; increased during World War II.
4. The SS–164 had a single 3-inch gun.

The S-1 (SS-105) prepares to flood down to launch an XS-1 floatplane during 1926 tests. She was the only U.S. submarine fitted to carry an aircraft until after World War II, when amphibious transport submarines were able to carry a small helicopter. (U.S. Navy)

Between the wars, S-boats became familiar sights off Panama, Hawaii, the Philippines, and China, as well as American ports. Here the S-32 (SS-137) is seen off Tsingato, China, in July 1928. (U.S. Navy)

weather prevented divers from going down. Soon the men in the stern compartment succumbed as their air was exhausted. Divers were able to communicate with those in the bow compartment, but weather and other problems prevented raising the S-4 until mid-March. In all, forty men died in the submarine. But her loss led to innovations in submarine escape and rescue which would save many lives in the future.

There were more S-boat accidents. Still, the submarines operated and provided the U.S. Navy with an effective force based at ports in the United States as well as in the Canal Zone and in the Philippines. One of the boats, the S-1, achieved a unique distinction as the U.S. Navy's only aircraft-carrying submarine.

There was considerable interest in increasing the search range of submarines by having them carry small aircraft that could be launched from the water's surface. During 1922–24 the Navy purchased a total of fourteen small aircraft intended to be carried aboard small ships, including submarines. The S-1 was fitted with a steel cylinder aft of her conning tower and during October–November 1923 she carried out tests with a Martin MS-1 float plane. No flights were made because it took four hours to assemble the aircraft on the submarine's narrow deck.

In 1926 the S-1 was again used for aircraft experiments and a Cox–Klemin XS-1 was employed. Upon the submarine's surfacing the aircraft was withdrawn from the hangar, assembled, and the submarine flooded down aft to float off the aircraft. The plane could be assembled and launched in only twelve minutes and recovered and stowed in the hanger in only thirteen. Again in 1932 the S-1 was used in experiments with aircraft, but a plan to equip nine U.S. submarines with aircraft was never carried out. (Britain, France, and Japan conducted similar experiments, and the last navy used submarine-launched aircraft during World War II.)

Post-World War I submarine designs grew in size, following European practices and taking advantage of information gleaned from six former German U-boats brought

An officer supervises the assembly of a Martin MS-1 floatplane aboard the S-1 during the 1923 tests. Because it took so long to prepare the aircraft for flight and then stow it after a flight, it was of little practical use. The 1926 tests were more successful as were those of 1931, but no operational deployment followed in the U.S. fleet. (U.S. Navy).

Several S-boats were lost through accidents, among them the S-51 (SS-162), rammed and sunk by a merchant ship off Block Island, Rhode Island, on the night of September 25, 1925. There were but three survivors from her crew of thirty-six. Her remains were raised on June 5, 1926, and towed into port. She is shown here in a dry dock; the large cylinders are pontoons used in her salvage. (U.S. Navy)

An MS-1 floatplane returns to the S-1 during the October 1923 tests. The sailors at right, who seem to be walking on water, are actually on the stern of the submarine which is barely awash. (U.S. Navy)

The *Bass* after her conversion to a cargo submarine at the Philadelphia Navy Yard in 1942-43. The conversion of these B-boats to that role was personally directed by President Roosevelt, who was apparently impressed by the use of submarines in supply runs to the Philippines. The deck guns, forward torpedo tubes, and after diesels were removed, among other changes. (U.S. Navy)

across the Atlantic after the war by American crews. (All were later sunk as targets, one in Lake Michigan and the others off the Atlantic coast.) Meanwhile Emory S. Land, a brilliant naval constructor, visited German and Austrian submarines and related activities, gathering information for future U.S. submarine designs.

The first postwar American submarines were the T-boats, "fleet" submarines authorized before U.S. entry into the war, but not laid down until 1920. All previous U.S. submarines except for the Navy-designed S-boats (i.e., S-3 type) were designed by commercial firms according to certain Navy-dictated specifications. The three T-boats were completed in 1920 and all subsequent fleet submarines were Navy-designed. The T-boats were the first U.S. submarines with a surface displacement of over 1,000 tons. They were not particularly successful, suffering from engine problems and poor seakeeping qualities. The submarines were laid up after a brief operational career and scrapped in 1930 along with several older boats in accordance with the London Naval Treaty.

The trend toward larger submarines was reflected in the next three submarine classes—the first of the so-called V-boats. All were originally assigned letter-number names in the V series, but were better known by their later names, with each class's names beginning with the same letter.

Thus the first V-boats were letter-named the *Barracuda*, *Bass*, and *Bonita* (SS-163 to -165). These large, 2,000-ton, 341½-foot submarines, completed from 1924 on, incorporated few lessons of submarine operations during the war. They had a bulbous bow, with the forward engine room placed forward of the conning tower and control room, bow and stern torpedo rooms, and two deck levels except in their forward and after torpedo rooms. Many other unusual features were found in those boats, including access hatch chambers that could be flooded and then drained to serve as escape chambers for the crew.

These boats also had limited success, being difficult to maneuver and also being ham-

The three B-boats: From left the
Bass (SS-164), *Barracuda* (SS-163),
and *Bonita* (SS-165) alongside the
submarine tender *Argonne* (AS-10)
at San Diego in December 1927.
Their bulbous bows had a stem
anchor, giving them a strange,
almost shark-like appearance. The
boats were complex, awkward, and
not particularly successful. During
World War II they were converted
to cargo submarines, but were not
used operationally. (U.S. Navy)

The *Bass* in dry dock at the Mare Island Navy Yard in the 1930s. Note her hull lines; the four torpedo-tube openings are low in the bow, below the canvas in front of the submarine; barely visible, aft of the name *Bass*, her diving planes are rigged out. (U.S. Navy)

The stern of the *Argonaut* (SM-1) just before launching in November 1927 at the Portsmouth Navy Yard. The two openings for her mine rails are just visible at her squared-off stern, just below the color change. One of the largest submarines of the time, the *Argonaut* was the only U.S. underseas craft built specifically as a minelayer. (U.S. Navy)

pered by their internal arrangement. They were laid up in 1937 and returned to service in wartime only for conversion to cargo submarines (redesignated APS-2 to -4). Their forward torpedo tubes and two (of four) engines were removed for cargo space, but even in this role the B-boats were failures.

More successful were the next three "giants"—the *Argonaut* and the two N-boats. The *Argonaut*, 2,710 tons on the surface and 381 feet overall, was the largest submarine built by the United States until after World War II. She was also the only U.S. submarine designed specifically for laying mines, having internal space for sixty Mark XI mines in addition to her four forward torpedo tubes. (Mines could also be launched from the torpedo tubes.) Her mine-laying role, for which she was re-designated SM-1 in place of SS-166, was unpopular because of the awkward minelaying arrangements and the U.S. Navy's limited interest in that mission.

During World War II the *Argonaut* was employed as a troop transport (APS-1), fitted to carry 120 Marines. She was used in this role to help raid Makin Island in 1942 along with the two N-boats. Like the N-boats, the *Argonaut* had two 6-inch deck guns, the largest guns ever fitted in U.S. submarines. Large and awkward to maneuver, the *Argonaut* had limited effectiveness as a patrol submarine. She was sunk by Japanese anti-submarine forces in 1943 with 105 officers and enlisted men on board, the most lost in any American submarine until the *Thresher* (SSN-593) disaster of 1963.

The *Narwhal* (SS-167) and *Nautilus* (SS-168) were almost as large, displacing 2,730 tons on the surface with an overall length of 370½ feet. Similar to the *Argonaut* except for the minelaying facilities, the N-boats were also awkward to maneuver, slow to dive, and slow on the surface. Still, they were useful boats; the *Nautilus* was modified to carry 19,000 gallons of aviation fuel for refueling seaplanes, a role she carried out before American entry in World War II. During the war they were used operationally, and both

The *Narwhal* (SS-167), first of two large N-boats, at sea in her pre-war configuration. Note the large 6-inch guns; with the *Argonaut*, these submarines had the heaviest gun batteries of any U.S. submarines. Their most significant war service was carrying troops on raids against Japanese-held islands. (U.S. Navy)

carried troops on the 1942 raid against Makin Island.

(By comparison, the largest foreign submarines of the between-war era were those of the British M class, completed in 1918-20, which displaced 1,650 tons and originally mounted a 12-inch gun; the later British X-1 of 3,050 tons armed with two gun mounts, each with twin 5.2-inch guns; and the French "underwater cruiser" *Surcouf* of 2,880 tons with a pair of 8-inch guns plus a hangar for carrying a seaplane. All also had torpedo tubes.)

After the large *Argonaut* and N-boats, the U.S. Navy shifted to smaller designs. This was a reaction to the high costs of the larger submarines. The first of these smaller submarines was the *Dolphin* (SS-169), which gave up the V-7 name while still on the building ways. When completed in 1932 the *Dolphin* showed the characteristic clean lines and other features of the Navy's later fleet submarines.

Forward, behind the *Dolphin*'s sharp prow, were the openings for four bow torpedo tubes and a pair of tubes was fitted in the stern. The internal arrangement set the standard for later U.S. submarines: first came the forward torpedo room, with reload torpedoes and bunks for the crew; next came the "officers' country," with berthing for the seven officers; then the control room, located below the conning tower; next the crew's quarters with bunks for most of the fifty-five sailors; the galley; then the engine room, followed by the maneuvering room where the engines were controlled; and finally, the after torpedo rooms. Between the torpedo room and engine room there was a lower level for the submarine's large wet-cell batteries, stores, and auxiliary machinery.

The last of the nine V series were the *Cachalot* and *Cuttlefish* (SS-170 and -171), completed in 1933-34. They were similar to the *Dolphin*, but slightly larger. All of the previous V-boats were built at the Portsmouth Navy Yard except for the *Nautilus*, built at the Mare Island Navy Yard off San Francisco Bay. The *Cachalot* was also built at Portsmouth; but the *Cuttlefish* was awarded

The clipper-bow submarine tender *Holland* (AS-3) at San Diego about 1930 with two of the B-boats and four S-boats moored alongside. Tenders supported submarines in U.S. ports as well as overseas, with the *Holland* having served as a mother ship to submarines from 1926 until 1945, when she was converted to an engine repair ship (ARG-18). (U.S. Navy)

to Electric Boat at Groton, the first submarines built there for the U.S. Navy since the S-boats. Due to the Electric Boat design modifications, the *Cuttlefish* had a separate mess compartment for the crew, separating the eating and sleeping spaces, a feature previously found only in the three largest U.S. submarines. There were other improvements in the EB design as well.

These boats were successful, but their speed and endurance would prove too limited for wartime operations in the Pacific. The next class remedied these limitations, bringing into being the U.S. fleet submarine.

The lone D-class submarine, the *Dolphin* (SS-169), was a significant reduction in size from her predecessors, reversing a design trend. She was not a particularly successful boat and was used mainly for training when war broke out. (U.S. Navy)

The *Cachalot* (S-170), shown here on August 23, 1935, and her sister ship *Cuttlefish* (SS-171), were the last of the so-called V-boats (although their actual pendant numbers were C-1 and C-2). They and the *Dolphin* were very short-range submarines. The C-boats each made three early war patrols and were then relegated to training duties. The *Cuttlefish* was the first American submarine to be fitted with air conditioning. (U.S. Navy)

A sailor demonstrates the Momsen escape lung aboard the *Narwhal*. The device could allow men to flood a compartment or use the escape chambers of a stricken submarine to escape to the surface without outside assistance—if the depth was not greater than about 200 feet. (U.S. Navy)

4. THE FLEET BOATS

"The year 1931 marked a watershed in submarine development. Inhibitions of the past seem to have been swept away, leaving a clear field for the pursuit of new ideas." Thus wrote Commander John D. Alden in his excellent study, *The Fleet Submarine in the U.S. Navy*. Those new ideas, sponsored by forward-looking naval engineers, resulted in the U.S. submarines launched from 1935 onward. The "fleet boats" served the United States ably in the Pacific during World War II, and made up much of the postwar submarine forces for the U.S. Navy and several foreign fleets.

Beginning with the *Porpoise* (SS-172), launched in 1935, these submarines were approximately 300 feet in length. Appearance and internal arrangements were similar to the *Cuttlefish*. Propulsion was provided by four large diesels while on the surface and four battery-powered electric motors while underwater. They had all-electric drive with the diesel engines connected to electric generators rather than to the propellers.

The *Porpoise* had six torpedo tubes, four forward and two aft, with ten reloads carried in her torpedo rooms for a total of sixteen fish. (During the war the *Porpoise* and some other submarines built between the wars had a pair of deck tubes also installed; these could not be reloaded from within the submarine.) The *Salmon* (SS-182), launched in 1937, increased the number of stern tubes to four, while the *Tambor* (SS-198) of 1939 had six bow tubes, for a total of ten. This became the standard for the fleet submarines, with fourteen reloads giving the fleet submarines a total punch of twenty-four torpedoes.

Deck guns were also reconsidered. The 3-inch/50-caliber deck gun mounted by most submarines in the 1930s was of minimal value. Many submarines favored a 5-inch gun that could be used against surface craft and aircraft, but none was yet in existence. Nevertheless, as an astute hedge for the future, the submarines were constructed with a deck foundation strong enough to carry the 5-inch gun, even though no "wet" mount was

The new S-boats were slightly faster than the previous P-class with two more stern torpedo tubes. This is the *Salmon* (SS-182) at sea on December 29, 1937. (U.S. Navy)

The *Marlin* (SS-205) was one of two experimental coastal submarines built during the fleet submarine period. Only the *Marlin* was modified during the war with a cut-down conning tower. Both units were used for training throughout the war. (U.S. Navy)

then available. A 3-inch/50 was installed in the first few fleet boats and later the 4-inch/50. The guns, removed from old S-boats, were fitted in the war-built submarines plus the earlier submarines when they were overhauled during the war. Some boats were also fitted with 5-inch/51 guns pending development of an improved weapon for submarines. Finally, in early 1944 the 5-inch/25 was available for submarines and rapidly installed in most U.S. undersea craft, with some submarines having mounts forward and aft of the conning tower.

Before World War II the submarines carried a couple of .30- to .50-caliber machine guns, either in the conning tower or watertight containers. These weapons could be mounted on pedestals to provide minimal protection against aircraft or small surface craft, but were inadequate in range and killing power. From 1943 on, U.S. submarines were fitted with single- or twin-barrel 20-mm Oerlikon cannons, and starting the following year with the potent 40-mm Bofors cannon. The 20s fired some 450 rounds per minute from drumlike magazines, while the 40-mm guns were hand loaded with four-round clips.

By the end of World War II some fleet submarines had two 5-inch, two 40-mm, and a couple of 20-mm weapons, permitting them to outgun many patrol boats and even destroyer escorts. (Also carried were a couple of .50-caliber machine guns plus rifles—including the BAR or Browning Automatic Rifle—pistols, and Thompson submachine guns.)

But the main punch of the submarines would be the torpedo, and the early, problem-prone torpedoes were used well into the war. From June 1943 onward the Mark 18 became the principal U.S. submarine torpedo. This was an electric-propelled fish, meaning that there were no steam-oxygen bubbles to create a wake as it sped toward an enemy ship at a speed of 29 knots. Targets could be engaged up to ranges of 4,000 yards, with the business end of the 20½-foot torpedo packing 595 pounds of high explosive known as TPX.

The fleet submarines could also lay mines

The conning-tower structure of the fleet boats was cut down during World War II, as shown here in this wartime view of the *Seal* (SS-183). She retains her 4-inch gun forward, and two mounts for 20-mm AA guns have been fitted forward and aft of her bridge. In addition, .50-caliber machine guns could be mounted on the bridge structure. (U.S. Navy)

TABLE 4. FLEET SUBMARINES

Hull Numbers	Number Completed	Class[1]	Launched	Displacement	Length Overall	Speed	Torpedo Tubes	Guns[2]	Crew	Depth
SS–172 to 181	10	P	1935–1937	1,310/1,960	301	17/8	4/2 21-in.	1 3-in.	50	250
SS–182 to 197	16	S	1937–1939	1,435/2,210	308	21/9	4/4 21-in.	1 4-in.	70	250
SS–198 to 203 SS–206 to 211	12	T	1939–1941	1,475/2,370	307¼	20/9	6/4 21-in.	1 3-in.	79	250
SS–204 to 205	2	Marlin	1940–1941	835/1,190	243¼	16/11	4/2 21-in.	1 3-in.	42	250
SS–212 to 284	73	Gato	1941–1943	1,525/2,415	311¾	20¼/10	6/4 21-in.	1 3/4-in.[3]	80	300
SS–285 to 416[4]	122[5]	Balao	1942–1947	1,525/2,415	311⅔	20¼/10	6/4 21-in.	1 3/4-in.[3]	80	400
SS–417 to 550[4]	31[6]	Tench	1944–1946	1,570/2,415	311⅔	20¼/10	6/4 21-in.	1 5-in.	81	400

1. There were minor differences in characteristics within the various classes.
2. Increased in most submarines during World War II.
3. Designed armament was one 3-inch or 4-inch gun; most eventually fitted with one or two 5-inch/25 single-purpose guns, plus lighter weapons.
4. Some units in class were cancelled or not completed.
5. One submarine completed in 1949 to GUPPY configuration.
6. Four submarines completed 1949–1950 to GUPPY configuration.

The *Perch* (SS-176) was one of the ten P-boats launched 1935-37, the first of the fleet boats that evolved into the two basic submarine designs that would be mass-produced during World War II. Note the pre-war conning tower shape, ship bow for surface performance, and P-5 pendant number. (U.S. Navy)

The McCann rescue chamber. The lines provide lift, air, electricity, and communications from the surface ship. The hatch opens to the upper portion of the nine-ton chamber, with the lower compartment being open to the sea until sealed to a submarine's hatch and pumped dry. (U.S. Navy)

An unusual view of four fleet boats operating in formation with the Battle Force during a 1939 exercise. Hull numbers have replaced pendant numbers on their conning towers: the *Seal* (SS-183), *Salmon* (SS-182), *Sturgeon* (SS-187), and *Stingray* (SS-186). During actual operations the submarines would be many miles apart. (U.S. Navy)

through their torpedo tubes, and when World War II began the Navy had 1,200 of the Mark 10 and half that number of the Mark 12 for submarine use. The shortage of torpedoes led to submarine minelaying missions starting in October 1942, with the first submarine minefields laid off Bangkok, Siam, followed a few days later with mines laid off the coast of Indochina and subsequently in Japanese home waters.

The Mark 10 had the well-known Hertz horns—small, horn-like projections from the mine that would electrically detonate the mine when struck by a ship. The Mark 12 had a magnetic detonator. Only a few of the Mark 10s were used and they were additionally fitted with a magnetic detonator, while all of the Mark 12s were laid. More types of mines were produced during the war. However, the submariners did not like using mines. When they did, fewer torpedoes could be carried, and torpedo hits could at least be seen, recorded, and credited to the submarine's record. Mines—the weapons that wait—might or might not sink a ship days or weeks after being planted, and submariners rarely knew the results of their work.

Radar, sonar, and warning devices also became important weapons during the war (see Chapter 5). All required highly trained personnel, and the submarine force soon became an elite within the Navy. All officers and enlisted men went through submarine school at New London. Unlike aviators, who were awarded wings after graduating from flight school, a New London graduate went to sea and qualified in a boat before being awarded his coveted dolphin insignia—gold if an enlisted man and silver if an officer.

The complexity of a submarine led to most of the enlisted men being "rated," that is, trained in a specific field. There were few unrated seamen aboard the submarines. The commanding officer, normally a lieutenant commander, and almost all of the other officers were Naval Academy graduates until the outbreak of the war. Then, as new boats were produced at a prodigious rate, increasing numbers of reserve officers entered the

The tug *Wandank* (AT-26), left, and submarine rescue vessel *Falcon* (ASR-2) moor above the sunken submarine *Squalus* (SS-192) in May 1939. Several small boats are in the choppy waters off Portsmouth. A McCann rescue chamber can be seen on the *Falcon*'s fantail. Note the fish emblem on her bow. (U.S. Navy)

The bow of the stricken *Squalus* breaks water, rising twenty feet above the surface at a 60-degree angle. But she slid out of her lifting chains as this photo was taken on July 13, 1939, and fell back to the ocean floor. She was finally raised in August and towed to the Portsmouth Navy Yard for rehabilitation. (U.S. Navy)

submarines' wardrooms. During the war the submarine commanders were generally in their early thirties, with their officers ranging from perhaps twenty-one up to their own age. The other officers were the executive officer, who also served as navigator, the chief engineer, torpedo and gunnery officer, communications officer, commissary officer, and their assistants—making up a wardroom of eight or nine officers.

Except for the captain, the officers and men were divided into three sections or watches, with one watch operating the boat, one off-duty and the third working on their "normal" assignments—maintaining torpedoes, cleaning up, etc. The sections normally rotated to operate the submarine while cruising. When "battle stations" was ordered, all crewmen manned their battle stations—torpedo or surface (guns). Each man had a specific position which he took, regardless of time of his watch section.

During the 1930s the Navy built a succession of fleet-type submarines, employing the Portsmouth and Mare Island navy yards, and the Electric Boat yard. The *Peto* (SS-265) was laid down in June 1941, introducing the Manitowoc Shipbuilding Company in Wisconsin to submarine construction. Because the yard was located on a river, its submarines were side-launched. After completion they were tested to operating depth in Lake Michigan. They were then towed to Lockport, Illinois and were placed on a floating dry dock for transport down the Mississippi River to New Orleans and the sea. Manitowoc completed twenty-eight submarines during World War II. Another private yard brought into the submarine picture was Cramp Shipbuilding Company in Philadelphia. This yard was closed from 1926 until 1940, when it reopened and was given a contract for twelve submarines. The sixth U.S. shipyard to construct submarines was the Navy Yard at Boston, which delivered four submarines during the war.

In all, the shipyards produced thirty-eight fleet-type submarines, from the *Porpoise* through the *Gudgeon* (SS-211), which joined the fleet in commissioning ceremonies in April 1941. There were also two small submarines, the *Mackerel* (SS-204) and *Marlin* (SS-205), both completed in 1941. These 800-ton boats, the smallest U.S. submarines since 1918, were experimental and no more were built during the war. Both operated along the Atlantic coast during the war, employed in training and research (although the *Mackerel* did have an inconclusive brush with a U-boat).

One fleet boat, the SS-192, had two names due to a tragic accident. Commissioned as the USS *Squalus* on March 1, 1939, that May the submarine was on diving trials off Portsmouth, New Hampshire. After successfully completed eighteen dives she went down again on the morning of May 23. As she disappeared beneath the waves the submarine's main induction valve failed to close. The inrushing water weighted her down, sending the submarine and fifty-nine men in her crashing to the bottom, 242 feet down. The after portion of the submarine flooded, killing the twenty-six men trapped in the engine and after torpedo rooms. Her designed operating depth was 250 feet, plus the 50-percent safety to "crush" depth. Thirty-three men in the control room and forward sections of the submarine were able to close off the watertight door to the flooded compartments.

The earlier submarine disasters had led to developments of submarine escape and rescue devices. *Escape* meant that the men in the submarine got out and to the surface on their own, using the emergency breathing devices which submarines carried. If a submarine was sunk but not fully flooded, the survivors could float to the surface. This scheme was used during the war on several occasions. But the escape "lungs" could not be used at the *Squalus*'s depth.

At deeper depths—where the *Squalus* rested—*rescue* was necessary, using the McCann rescue chamber. This was a steel diving bell that could hold seven survivors plus an operator. First divers from surface ships would attach a cable to the stricken submarine. Then the cable would be attached to the bell, which could be winched

Rebuilt and ready for war: this is
how the *Squalus* appeared during
World War II, rebuilt and renamed
Sailfish (still SS-192). She would
make twelve war patrols in the
Pacific through 1944, and then spend
the last year of the war as a training
ship. (U.S. Navy)

down to the submarine's deck, "mating" with one of the escape hatches. The bell's hatch could then be opened to permit access to the submarine.

Under arduous conditions, divers fastened the cable to the *Squalus* and in four trips the thirty-three survivors were brought to the surface. On the last trip, the cable jammed and the final group of eight *Squalus* men and the two operators spent a harrowing time suspended between surface and submarine.

Later the *Squalus* was refloated in the most difficult U.S. salvage operation to that date. She was finally towed triumphantly into Portsmouth on September 13, 1939. After extensive reconditioning the SS-192 was recommissioned as the USS *Sailfish* on May 15, 1940. As the *Sailfish* she would make twelve war patrols, sinking seven Japanese ships—including a 20,000-ton escort aircraft carrier—and damaging several others.

Improvements in the fleet boats continued up to the *Gato* (SS-212), commissioned on the last day of 1941. This Electric Boat-built submarine was the "standard" fleet type that would be constructed during the war. She differed in several respects from the earlier fleet boats and had an operating depth of 300 feet, the first U.S. submarine with that capability. The *Gato* design was "frozen" and the boats completed during the war were identical in most major respects, with the *Balao* (SS-285) and later boats having a 400-foot operating depth.

Increased operating depths meant that it took longer for anti-submarine depth charges to plummet down to the submarine, giving it more time to move away. And, the hull of a deeper-diving submarine offered more protection from depth charges when at shallower depths. Apparently the Japanese did not realize that the later war-built submarines could dive deeper. However, in June 1943, a Congressman returning from the war zone may have given away the secret to the Japanese. According to Clay Blair's historical study *Submarine Victory*, "he said, in effect, Don't worry about our submarines; the Japanese are setting their depth charges too shallow. Incredibly, the press associations sent this story over their wires, and many newspapers . . . thoughtlessly published it."

Vice Admiral Charles Lockwood, commander of U.S. submarines in the Pacific for most of the war, is cited as declaring that after Congressman Andrew Jackson May's statement the Japanese set their deep charges to explode at deeper depths. Lockwood himself wrote: "I consider that indiscretion cost us ten submarines and 600 officers and men."*

As war erupted in the Pacific with the Japanese assaults on China in the 1930s, and then in Europe with Germany's invasion of Poland, then Scandinavia and western Europe, there were major increases in U.S. shipbuilding programs. When the Japanese attacked Pearl Harbor on December 7, 1941, the U.S. Navy had 111 submarines in commission and another 73 fleet boats under construction or on order. Within days of the Pearl Harbor attack still more building contracts for submarines would be awarded as submarines became one of the primary American weapons in the Pacific War.

---

*The deepest diving Japanese submarines during the war had an operational depth of 355 feet, with most being rated less capable. Some German U-boats had 650-foot ratings, and some successfully returned from dives to half-again that depth.

Hidden under the scaffolding is the *Silversides* (SS-236), under construction at the Mare Island Navy Yard near San Francisco. This photo was taken on July 1, 1941, about two months before the submarine was launched. Submarines were the most complicated warships to build, in part because of the cramped confines of their hull and the vast amount of equipment and fittings stuffed into them. (U.S. Navy)

5. EXECUTE UNRESTRICTED... SUBMARINE WARFARE

At 7:55 on the morning of December 7, 1941, aircraft from six Japanese carriers bombed the U.S. naval base at Pearl Harbor, Hawaii, plunging the United States into World War II. Shortly after the attack on Pearl Harbor, the Chief of Naval Operations in Washington flashed the following to all U.S. naval forces: EXECUTE UNRESTRICTED AIR AND SUBMARINE WARFARE AGAINST JAPAN. At the moment of the attack five U.S. submarines were at sea to the west of Hawaii, two on patrol off the island of Midway at the northwestern extremity of the Hawaiian chain, two off Wake Island in the mid-Pacific, and another returning from a forty-three-day patrol off Midway.

The day of the Pearl Harbor attack, the Japanese Navy began bombing attacks on Wake Island, which was held by a handful of U.S. Marines and sailors. During the night of December 8-9 (one day later than U.S. time) the submarine *Tambor* (SS-198), patrolling off Wake, sighted Japanese warships but was unable to close for an attack. The following night the *Triton* (SS-201) also sighted warships off Wake and, after three hours of hide-and-seek maneuvers with enemy ships, fired four torpedoes at one of the pursuing Japanese ships. A single explosion was heard in this first U.S. submarine attack of the war, and the *Triton* was credited with damaging a Japanese ship.

The United States began the war with 111 submarines in commission and another 73 under construction. Of the operational submarines, 51 were in the Pacific on December 7—29 of them with the Asiatic Fleet based in the Philippines and 22 assigned to the Pacific Fleet based at Pearl Harbor. When the Japanese struck Pearl there were seven submarines at the submarine base, just northeast of "battleship row." Another was engaged in local operations, and several were on the West Coast of the United States undergoing overhaul or training, or were in transit between Pearl and the mainland.

When the Japanese bombs fell on Pearl Harbor the orders to commence unrestricted

The victor returns: a battle-scarred
fleet submarine returns to Pearl Harbor after a patrol in enemy waters
with miniature Japanese flags flying
from her periscopes to indicate
enemy ships believed sunk. She will
tie up at the Pearl submarine base,
alongside the recently returned sub
in foreground. The returning boat is
the *Tinosa* (SS-283), which according
to postwar records sank sixteen
Japanese ships of 64,000 tons. Note
the 5-inch/25-caliber "wet" gun
mount in foreground, the standard
deck gun in the latter stages of the
war. (U.S. Navy)

Amidst the wreckage of Pearl Harbor, Admiral Chester W. Nimitz took command of the Pacific Fleet aboard the submarine *Grayling* (SS-209) in a brief ceremony on December 31, 1941. Nimitz was a veteran submarine officer, with his first assignment being concurrent command of the First Submarine Flotilla and the *Plunger* (SS-2) in 1909. Moored forward of the *Grayling* at the Pearl submarine base was the recently converted tender *Pelias* (AS-14). (U.S. Navy)

Early in the war, U.S. submarines began carrying ammunition and other supplies to the beleaguered Philippines. The submarines carried out torpedoes from the Cavite Navy Yard, and then technicians and nurses from Corregidor. But the *Trout* (SS-202) also carried out the Philippine Commonwealth treasury—two tons of gold bars and eighteen tons of silver pesos—shown here being transferred to the cruiser *Detroit* (CL-8) at Pearl Harbor after the mission. (U.S. Navy)

submarine warfare meant that any ship flying the Japanese flag—warship or merchantman—was to be attacked. The prewar plans had envisioned submarines being used mainly to scout ahead of the battle fleet, reporting the enemy's movements and slowing down his ships with torpedo attacks. But with much of the battle fleet lying shattered at the shallow bottom of Pearl Harbor, the submarine's role changed.

The first blood was drawn by a United States submarine on December 16 when the *Swordfish* (SS-193) torpedoed and sank an 8,662-ton Japanese freighter off the coast of Indochina. This was the first confirmed kill of the war by a United States sub. Although several others had made attacks and scored hits, the stricken ships did not sink. Time and time again, the submarines were making "perfect" shots without results. Typical of these frustrating experiences was that of the *Tinosa* under Lieutenant Commander L. R. Daspit.

The *Tinosa* encountered the Japanese *Tonan Maru No. 3*, a 19,262-ton floating whale factory that had been converted to a tanker. She was one of Japan's largest merchant ships and a coveted target. The *Tinosa* had sixteen torpedoes on board. "Dan" Daspit, later a vice admiral, recalled that he attacked the ship with a spread of four torpedoes. Two of them hit near the tanker's stern, but did not explode. The ship kept going and the *Tinosa* fired her two remaining bow tubes at the tanker. These hit, exploded, and the big Maru stopped; her propellers had been damaged.

"There she lay, dead in the water," Daspit later related, "but with guns which considerably outranged our small 3-inch gun. She was unescorted and the chances that she could hit us with gunfire when her only target was a periscope, infrequently exposed, were small. We, therefore, took the time deliberately to fire all but one of our remaining torpedoes. They were all good, solid hits, and all duds!" Fifteen torpedoes had been fired and twelve or thirteen had hit the target.

This took place in July of 1943, more than a year and a half after the war in the Pacific

Another "sugar" boat that saw action in the war was the S-42 (SS-153), shown here with her crew on deck, returning to the advanced U.S. submarine base at Brisbane, Australia. She sank the 4,400-ton Japanese minelayer *Okinoshima* off New Ireland in May 1942. (U.S. Navy)

Reconnaissance and other special missions, as well as attacks against enemy shipping, took U.S. submarines into all corners of the Japanese empire during the war. This periscope view of Mount Fujiyama was snapped by the *Trigger* (SS-237). (U.S. Navy)

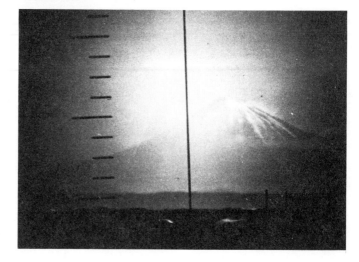

While the fleet submarines were the highly publicized warriors of World War II, the older submarines, especially the S-boats, also served, especially in the Far Eastern and Alaskan areas. This is the S-47 (SS-158) as modified during the war. A platform has been added to her conning tower for a 20-mm gun; a 3-inch/50-caliber gun has been fitted; and radars have been installed. At far left is a *New Mexico*-class battleship. (U.S. Navy)

This posed photo for "the folks back home" shows sailors sharing the forward torpedo room of a submarine with a pair of "fish"—21 inches in diameter, almost 21 feet long, and weighing about a ton. The war-built *Gato* (SS-212) and *Balao* (SS-285) classes had ten torpedo tubes with a total "loadout" of twenty-four torpedoes. (U.S. Navy)

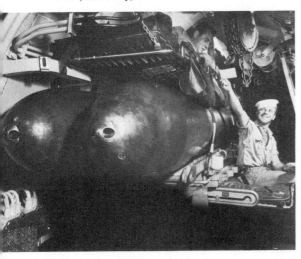

started! But once the torpedo malfunctions were corrected, the Japanese ships started going down. (The *Tinosa* herself later sank sixteen merchant ships.)

Another submarine with similar experiences with faulty torpedoes was the *Gudgeon* (SS-211), which arrived at Pearl Harbor on December 10 from the mainland. One of the newest submarines in the fleet, she loaded supplies at Pearl and began her first war patrol twenty-four hours later. The submarine headed westward, for the Bungo Suido Strait, between the Japanese home islands of Kyushu and Shikoku. Several times she fired torpedoes at enemy ships without results.

But the *Gudgeon*'s luck changed late on January 26, when a message was received from ComSubPac—Commander Submarines Pacific Fleet—that one of the Japanese submarines that had just shelled Midway Island would pass across the track of the U.S. sub, returning from patrol in Japanese home waters without a single score. Early the next morning the *Gudgeon*'s sonar operator detected propeller sounds. A periscope check on the sound contact's bearing revealed a large Japanese submarine cutting through the surface at about 15 knots.

Only ten minutes later, in a textbook exercise, the *Gudgeon* launched three torpedoes at the surfaced I-173. Moments later the Imperial Japanese Navy lost a 1,785-ton submarine. This was the first enemy warship to be sunk by a U.S. submarine during the war. Despite faulty torpedoes early in the war, American submarines sank 55 percent of the total merchant tonnage and 29 percent of the warships lost by the Japanese during the war. Yet the men who sailed the submarines numbered only 1.6 percent of the entire U.S. Navy.

Japan had gone to war against the United States primarily to gain access to the petroleum and other resources of Southeast Asia, and to fight the war in China without interference from the U.S. fleet. U.S. submarines sank 1,178 Japanese merchant ships of over 500 gross tons, a total tonnage of over five million. These merchant losses literally starved Japan out of the war. In addition,

Score another one for the submarine force. A Japanese merchant ship goes down after being struck by torpedoes from a U.S. submarine. Submarines, coupled with sea mines laid by B-29s in the final stages of the war, isolated the Japanese homeland from the remaining overseas empire, cutting off the Japanese population and industry from the food and raw materials needed to continue the war. (U.S. Navy)

Submarines carried out a number of reconnaissance landings and raids against Japanese-held islands in the Pacific. The large *Argonaut* transported 121 Marines and the *Nautilus* 90 for the August 1942 raid on Makin Island in the Gilbert group. Here Marines exercise near a 6-inch/53-caliber deck gun on the *Nautilus*, en route to the successful raid. The Marines returned to Makin and nearby Tarawa in November 1943 in a bloody assault to capture the islands. (U.S. Navy)

Another two-submarine raid occurred on May 11, 1943, when the *Nautilus* and *Narwhal* landed Army Rangers on Attu as part of a major U.S. assault on that Aleutian isle. Here the *Nautilus* offloads Rangers into rubber boats during a rehearsal at Dutch Harbor, Alaska, on April 30. Reload torpedoes and other equipment were removed from these submarines to enable them to each carry just over 100 troops for the Attu raid. (U.S. Navy)

A new submarine about to go to sea on trials. This is the *Scorpion* (SS-278), commissioned shortly before this photo was taken of her going to sea in December 1942. She departed Pearl Harbor on her first war patrol the following April. The 3-inch/50-caliber gun shown here was later replaced by a 4-inch/50. The "jack" flying at the *Scorpion*'s bow indicates she is not yet underway. (U.S. Navy)

The limited water area at Manitowoc, Wisconsin, led to those inland-built submarines being side-launched, as the *Pogy* (SS-266) is shown here when she entered the water on June 23, 1942. (U.S. Navy)

these same submarines sank 214 naval vessels. Among them were a battleship, four fleet aircraft carriers, four escort carriers, twelve cruisers, forty-two destroyers, and twenty-three submarines. Three of the Japanese submarines were sunk by the USS *Batfish* (SS-310) in a four-day period while three of the destroyers went down to torpedoes from the *Harder* (SS-257), also in a four-day period! (The *Harder* also sank another destroyer and two anti-submarine frigates before she succumbed to enemy action in early 1945.) Two destroyers were sunk on the same day by the *Flasher* (SS-249) while the submarine *Sealion* (SS-315) got the battleship *Kongo* and a destroyer in a single attack. The biggest prize of all, the 68,059-ton aircraft carrier *Shinano*, went down to torpedoes from the submarine *Archerfish* (SS-311). The giant flattop, the largest aircraft carrier to be built until the U.S. nuclear carriers of the postwar era, was sunk on her maiden voyage, just ten days after she was commissioned.

In mid-1942 the Navy began providing radar to submarines, at first surface-search radar that could detect ships at night and in fog, providing range and bearing information to the TDC—Torpedo Data Computer—to permit attacks against unseen targets. This was followed by air-search radar, which together with warning devices that could detect radar in enemy aircraft, permitted submarines to operate on the surface, diving to avoid air attack with a greater measure of reliability than that provided by lookouts. The submarines were faster on the surface, and the broad Pacific involved long transit times to patrol areas. Because Japanese anti-submarine efforts were of limited effectiveness, U.S. subs could spend most of their time on the surface. Radar thus improved their effectiveness and made them less vulnerable to enemy attack.

Still another "weapon" available to U.S. submarines was radio intercept. At an early stage in the war the U.S. Navy was able to intercept and decipher Japanese operational codes. Thus, very often submarines could be

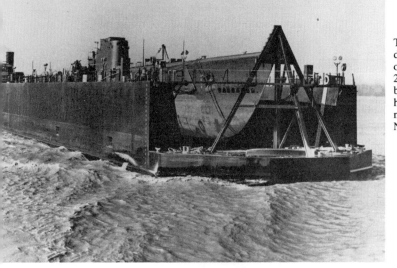

The Manitowoc boats were floated down the Mississippi for fitting out on the coast. This is the *Peto* (SS-265) in a floating dock, being pushed by tugs. Her periscopes and masts have not yet been installed, to permit passage under low bridges. (U.S. Navy)

Off to war: the *Drum* (SS-228) departs the San Francisco Navy Yard at Hunter's Point in July 1945. Note her heavy armament of two 5-inch/25-caliber guns, and a 40-mm mounted forward on the conning tower step. Additional 20-mm and .50-caliber guns will be carried into combat. Note the two periscope shears atop the conning tower, with a separate radar mast behind them. (U.S. Navy)

Off to war: the *Ronquil* (SS-396) crosses a placid sea. Note her heavy armament of two 5-inch/25-caliber guns and two 40-mm guns on conning tower steps; there are also 20-mm and .50-caliber guns. Note the two periscope shears atop the conning tower, with a separate radar mast behind them. (U.S. Navy)

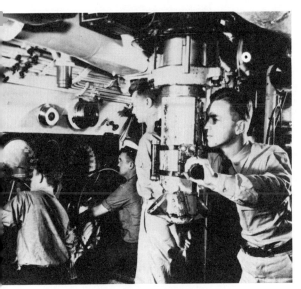

Students and veterans mix aboard this submarine being used in a training role at New London, Connecticut. The commanding officer is at the periscope in the control room. Beyond him a chief petty officer and another sailor operate the diving plane controls. Their depth gauges indicate that the boat is level with a depth of about 45 feet from keel to surface. (U.S. Navy)

A closeup of the conning tower of the *Hardhead* (SS-365). The two periscopes can be just seen extending from the twin shears. Behind them is a radar antenna and a retracted radio mast. The conning tower contained the attack center; the submarine was controlled from the control room, directly below the tower. In this April 1944 photo drum magazines are in both 20-mm cannon. Barely visible on the tower are mountings for machine guns. (U.S. Navy)

guided to convoys or to specific enemy ship tracks.

There were some efforts to coordinate U.S. submarines with fleet surface actions, as had been planned before Pearl Harbor. At the important carrier battle near Midway in June 1942 the eleven available U.S. submarines were formed into a barrier line to intercept the Japanese carriers. However, only one submarine made a contact and her single attack was ineffective. (Japanese submarines, employed in a similar manner, did sink a damaged U.S. carrier and the destroyer alongside her.)

Two years later, in the June 1944 carrier battle of the Marianas—the largest single fleet action of World War II—U.S. submarines were again deployed along the expected path of the Japanese warships. These subs were more successful, with two of nine Japanese carriers in the battle being sunk by their torpedoes.

As larger numbers of U.S. submarines became available, "wolf pack" tactics were initiated. This simply meant that several submarines would operate together in an area of probable enemy shipping, with coordinated attacks being more effective. A typical wolf-pack action took place off the coast of Formosa on July 30, 1944. The subs were the *Steelhead* (SS-280), *Parche* (SS-384), and *Hammerhead* (SS-364). Late that night a Japanese convoy was spotted. The *Steelhead* and *Parche* were in position to attack, and in the pre-dawn hours of July 31 they went roaring in. The *Steelhead* opened the action with a spread of six torpedoes aimed at a tanker and a large freighter. One torpedo was seen to hit the freighter and seconds later the tanker was hit. Four more torpedoes streaked from the *Steelhead*'s stern tubes at another freighter. Next the *Parche* joined the foray. Immediately a Japanese escort ship was after her and two more stood between the sub and the convoy. But the *Parche*'s skipper, Commander Lawson P. Ramage, evaded this deadly trio with skillful surface maneuvering and the *Parche* was among the flock of Japanese merchantmen. Two torpedoes fired at a freighter missed. Next, four

Fifty-two U.S. submarines did not return to port during World War II. This is the high-scoring *Darter* (SS-227), hard aground on Bombay Shoal off southwestern Palawan. Her crew has been taken off and she has been extensively shelled by the submarine *Nautilus* to prevent her capture by the Japanese. (U.S. Navy)

Submariners kept careful score of their attacks and alleged sinkings, some of which required recounting with postwar information available from Japanese files. Here miniature Japanese flags fly from the periscope shears of the *Batfish* as she returns to port in May 1945, while sailors aboard the *Plunger* (SS-179) display their battle flag in June 1943, probably while their boat is in the Sea of Japan. (U.S. Navy)

A diving officer supervises two enlisted men at the diving plane controls of the *Batfish* (SS-310). Note the maze of dials and pointers, further testimony to the complexity of submarine operation. The *Batfish* is unique in submarine history, having sunk three enemy undersea craft. (U.S. Navy)

A submarine loads torpedoes, ammunition, food, and other supplies for a combat patrol of several weeks at sea. As the war progressed, Guam was used as a forward submarine base, supplementing Pearl and Brisbane. Submarines could also top off their fuel supply at Midway. (U.S. Navy)

torpedoes were unleashed at an enemy tanker. All hit. Three more "fish" were aimed at a second tanker. Two hit.

The fury of the attack is best told in Commander Ramage's citation for the action: "A series of bow and stern torpedoes [were fired] to sink the leading tanker and damage the second one. Exposed by the light of bursting flares and bravely defiant of terrific shellfire passing close overhead, he struck again sinking a transport by two forward reloads. In the mounting fury of fire from the damaged and sinking tanker, he calmly ordered his men below, remaining on the bridge to fight it out with an enemy now disorganized and confused. Swift to act as a fast transport closed in to ram, [he] daringly swung the stern of the speeding *Parche* as she crossed the bow of the onrushing ship, clearing by less than 50 feet but placing his submarine in the deadly crossfire from the escorts on all sides and with the transport dead ahead. Undaunted, he sent three smashing down-the-throat bow shots to stop the target, then scored a killing hit as a climax to 46 minutes of violent action with the *Parche* and her valiant fighting company retiring victorious and unscathed." Commander Ramage's award for his action that night was the nation's highest: the Medal of Honor. He later became a vice admiral.

A few miles from the *Parche*'s battles, the *Steelhead* was attacking two ships, each receiving a four-torpedo attack. Both were hit and one was soon sinking, but an enemy plane drove the *Steelhead* off before she could finish off the second ship. In all, five large enemy merchant ships were sunk and many more damaged.

The submarine *Tautog* (SS-199) sank twenty-six Japanese ships to lead all U.S. submarines in the number of ships sent to the bottom. But the *Flasher*, which sank twenty-one, led in tonnage sunk with 100,231 tons, compared to the *Tautog*'s 72,606 tons.

In the Atlantic, six U.S. submarines operated in European waters during 1942. After the invasion of North Africa by Anglo–American forces that November, they were shifted to the Pacific, leaving the Atlantic–

TABLE 5. U.S. SUBMARINE LOSSES IN WORLD WAR II

Number	Name	Date Lost	Cause	Location	Fatalities
SS–195	Sealion	Dec. 10, 1941	Air attack	Cavite Navy Yard, Philippines	1
SS–141	S–36	Jan. 20, 1942	Stranding	Makassar Strait	0
SS–131	S–26	Jan. 24, 1942	Collision	Gulf of Panama	46
SS–174	Shark	Feb. 1942	Surface attack	Makassar Strait area	58
SS–176	Perch	Mar. 3, 1942	Surface attack	Java Sea	0 (9 died as prisoners)
SS–132	S–27	June 19, 1942	Stranding	Aleutians	0
SS–216	Grunion	July–Aug. 1942	Unknown	Aleutians	70
SS–144	S–39	Aug. 16, 1942	Stranding	Rossel Island	0
SS–166	Argonaut	Jan. 10, 1943	Surface attack	Solomon Sea	105
SS–219	Amberjack	Feb. 16, 1943	Air-surface attack	Solomon Sea	74
SS–207	Grampus	Mar. 1943	Surface attack	Coral Sea	71
SS–201	Triton	Mar. 15, 1943	Surface attack	off New Guinea	74
SS–177	Pickerel	Apr. 3, 1943	Surface attack	off Japan	74
SS–210	Grenadier	Apr. 22, 1943	Air attack	off Malay Peninsula	0 (4 died as prisoners)
SS–275	Runner	May–July 1943	Mine (?)	Western Pacific	78
SS–89	R–12	June 12, 1943	Flooding	off Key West, Florida	42
SS–209	Grayling	Aug.–Sep. 1943	Unknown	South China Sea	76
SS–181	Pompano	Aug.–Sep. 1943	Mine (?)	Western Pacific	76
SS–290	Cisco	Sep. 28, 1943	Air-surface attack (?)	Sulu Sea	76
SS–149	S–44	Oct. 7, 1943	Surface attack	Sea of Okhotsk	55
SS–238	Wahoo	Oct. 11, 1943	Air attack (?)	off Japan	80
SS–248	Dorado	Oct. 12, 1943	Unknown	off Atlantic coast	76
SS–226	Corvina	Nov. 16, 1943	Submarine attack	Caroline Islands	82
SS–191	Sculpin	Nov. 19, 1943	Surface attack	Caroline Islands	12 (51 more died as prisoners)
SS–289	Capelin	Dec. 9, 1943	Surface attack (?)	Celebes Sea	78
SS–278	Scorpion	Jan.–Feb. 1944	Mine (?)	East China Sea	76
SS–208	Grayback	Feb. 26, 1944	Air-surface attack	Western Pacific	80
SS–202	Trout	Feb. 1944	Surface attack (?)	Philippine Sea	81
SS–284	Tullibee	Mar. 26, 1944	Own torpedo (?)	Caroline Islands	79
SS–211	Gudgeon	May 12, 1944 (?)	Air-surface attack	Mariana Islands	78
SS–233	Herring	June 1, 1944	Surface attack	Kurile Islands	84
SS–361	Golet	June 14, 1944 (?)	Surface attack	off Japan	82
SS–132	S–28	July 4, 1944	Operational	Hawaiian Islands	50
SS–273	Robalo	July 26, 1944	Operational	South China Sea	78 (4 more died as prisoners)
SS–250	Flier	Aug. 13, 1944	Mine	South China Sea	78
SS–257	Harder	Aug. 24, 1944	Surface attack	South China Sea	79
SS–197	Seawolf	Oct. 3, 1944	U.S. forces (?)	off New Guinea	99
SS–227	Darter	Oct. 24, 1944	Stranding	off Palawan	0
SS–314	Shark	Oct.–Nov. 1944	Surface attack	off Formosa	87
SS–306	Tang	Oct. 24, 1944	Own torpedo	Formosa Strait	78
SS–294	Escolar	Sep.–Oct. 1944	Mine or surface attack (?)	Western Pacific	82
SS–218	Albacore	Nov. 7, 1944	Mine	off Japan	86
SS–215	Growler	Nov. 8, 1944	Surface attack (?)	South China Sea	85
SS–277	Scamp	Nov. 1944	Air-surface attack	off Japan	83
SS–193	Swordfish	Jan. 12, 1945	Surface attack (?)	off Okinawa	89
SS–316	Barbel	Feb. 4, 1945	Air attack	off Palawan	81
SS–369	Kete	Mar. 1945	Unknown	south of Japan	87
SS–237	Trigger	Mar. 1945	Air-surface attack	East China Sea	89
SS–279	Snook	Apr. 1945	Unknown	off Formosa	84
SS–371	Lagarto	May 3, 1945	Surface attack	Gulf of Siam	85
SS–223	Bonefish	June 18, 1945	Surface attack	off Japan	85
SS–332	Bullhead	Aug. 6, 1945	Air attack	off Bali	84

Japanese merchant shipping became scarce and there were fewer Japanese anti-submarine forces toward the end of the war. Thus, U.S. submarines increasingly used their deck guns to sink the smaller ships. Here submariners fire four-round clips of 40-mm ammunition at a target, while down on the main deck a 5-inch/25 is trained on the target. (U.S. Navy)

Decorations came for successful patrols and personal heroism. Medals and commendations are given to the crew of the *Batfish* at left while the men aboard the submarine in foreground take a break from business as usual. A band stands by on the pier at the Pearl Harbor submarine base. A wartime censor has drawn circles around the radar antennas on the two submarines' masts. (U.S. Navy)

Mediterranean theaters to British submarines. U.S. submarines were credited with only one kill, an anti-submarine trawler, in the Atlantic. It was the Pacific that provided the successful hunting grounds for American submarines.

But the American submarine successes in the Pacific were not without cost. The first loss was the *Sealion* (SS-195). During a Japanese air attack on the Cavite Navy Yard in the Philippines she was tied up between another submarine and a minesweeper. Almost simultaneously two bombs slammed into the *Sealion*. Crippled and partially sunk by the blasts, she was scuttled on Christmas Day 1941. Thus fell the first of fifty-two U.S. submarines lost in World War II. Of these thirty-six were definitely known to have been lost to Japanese military action—guns, bombs, mines, and depth charges, and one to a submarine's torpedoes. Ten others were lost in combat areas, either to enemy action or operationally. These include two believed lost when their own torpedoes malfunctioned and made circular runs, and four that were stranded in shallow water and subsequently destroyed. One U.S. submarine was sunk by an American destroyer and another by friendly aircraft. Of the four submarines lost in non-combat areas, one was sunk in a collision off Panama, two during training operations, and the fourth to unknown causes somewhere between New London and Panama. There is some belief that the last may have been sunk by a German U-boat that was herself sunk on the same patrol.

When the war ended in mid-August 1945 the U.S. Navy had 260 submarines in commission. Several of them were older craft, some O, R, and S boats of the World War I era relegated to training duties. But most were modern fleet boats, of which 202 had been delivered during the war, with many more on the building ways when the conflict ended.

After the war Vice Admiral Forrest Sherman, one of the U.S. Navy's most astute officers, wrote: "The danger inherent in any report confined to one aspect of the war is that it may mislead the reader into forgetting

Appearing like a band of pirates from out of the past, crewmen of the submarine *Lamprey* (SS-372) seek out junks, sampans, and barges supporting Japanese activities in the Western Pacific at the end of the war. The lack of effective Japanese ASW forces at war's end made sustained surface operations relatively safe for U.S. submarines. When these photos were taken, the *Lamprey* was in the Java Sea. (Commander John D. Alden)

The *Trigger* (SS-237), shown here in April 1942, was the top-scoring U.S. submarine in terms of tonnage, sinking eighteen ships for 86,552 tons before she herself was sunk by the Japanese on March 28, 1945. A Japanese pilot's report of the attack read: "Detected a submarine and bombed it. Ships also detected it, and depth-charged. Found oil pool, one to five miles in size, the next day." All eighty-nine men on board perished with the *Trigger*. (U.S. Navy)

that the conflict was won by a combination of ground, naval, and air forces, each of which carried its share of the common burden." In this regard, the submarine force was but one component of the massive American naval armada. But its accomplishments were significant, and out of all proportion to its size.

"Let pass safely" was the wording periodically sent by the Navy to submarines at sea, as messages announced a Japanese ship that had been given safe passage. The hospital ship shown here was one of them. However, the *Queenfish* (SS-393) did sink a Japanese ship that had carried supplies to Allied prisoners in Southeast Asia. No prisoners were on board when she was sunk in a radar-directed attack. The captain of the U.S. submarine was court-martialed for the action. (U.S. Navy)

Unfortunately, some U.S. submarines sank Japanese merchant ships not knowing that there were Allied prisoners on board. More than 2,000 Australian and British POWs were crammed into the holds of the *Rakuyo Maru* and *Kachidoki Maru* when they were sunk by U.S. submarines. Here the *Sealion* (SS-315), which sank the former ship, pulls survivors from a raft and from the oil-covered waters. (U.S. Navy)

U.S. submarines also proved invaluable in rescuing downed Allied aviators. The *Tigrone* (SS-419) set a record in 1945 when she rescued twenty-nine fliers in just five days. This U.S. submarine, within sight of the Japanese coast of Kyushu, is picking up a downed Army pilot (in circle) after a 1945 air strike against the Japanese home islands. (U.S. Navy)

Coming home: a fleet submarine comes alongside a pier after a long patrol. (U.S. Navy)

The world's three largest submarines, flying the Stars and Stripes in August 1945: Moored outboard of the U.S. submarine tender *Proteus* (AS-19) in Tokyo Bay are the ex-Japanese submarines I-400, I-401, I-402, completed in 1944–45. With an overall length of 402 ½ feet and a submerged displacement of 6,560 tons, the I-400s were the largest non-nuclear submarines constructed by any nation. They were designed to carry three seaplane bombers (plus components for a fourth) that could be launched from a deck catapult. (U.S. Navy)

After World War II the prewar fleet boats, and most of the war-built ones, were laid up in reserve, expended as targets for new weapons, or broken up for scrap. By early 1950 there were only seventy-three submarines in active service. This aerial photograph shows a part of the Pacific reserve fleet at Mare Island, California. A dozen submarines are mothballed among destroyers and mine, amphibious, and auxiliary ships. (U.S. Navy)

6. GUPPIES AND OTHER FISHES

The future of the U.S. Navy was uncertain after World War II. Despite the contribution of naval forces to the Allied victory over Germany and Japan, the nation's leaders questioned whether warships would be useful in the future. There was widespread assumption that the atomic bomb made all surface ships obsolete. There were no other fleets afloat—hostile or allied—that could effectively challenge even a single U.S. carrier task group. And U.S. submarines, which had made such a significant contribution to the war in the Pacific, would be without a mission of any sort because the United States' major postwar antagonist, the Soviet Union, had virtually no surface fleet or merchant marine. Many American political and military leaders believed, or at least hoped, that long-range bombers, at some future time carrying atomic bombs, would be sufficient military force to deter foreign aggression.

In an effort to determine the potential vulnerability of warships to atomic attack, the U.S. military services conducted atomic bomb tests against warships and other equipment at the Bikini Atoll in the Pacific in July 1946. Known as the Crossroads Project, the tests sought to obtain information on how well warships could survive and possibly continue fighting during an atomic attack.

A flotilla of U.S. ships as well as surrendered German and Japanese ships—a total of sixty-seven ships plus many landing craft—were moored at various distances from the target point. The target ships for the two atomic bomb detonations included eight submarines: the *Searaven* (SS-196), *Skipjack* (SS-184), *Tuna* (SS-203), *Dentuda* (SS-335), *Skate* (SS-305), *Apogon* (SS-308), *Parche* (SS-384) and *Pilotfish* (SS-386). The submarines were on the surface or submerged to predetermined depths, the latter being lowered by remote means.

In the first test, with an atomic bomb of about 20 kilotons power,* the weapon was dropped by a B-29 bomber with some twenty of the target ships located within one square

Among the weapons tested against submarines after the war were two atomic bombs at Bikini Atoll. Eight submarines were moored as targets in the two nuclear tests. This is the *Skate* (SS-305) after the nuclear air burst on July 1, 1946. She had been one-half mile from the explosion. Her superstructure and periscope were bent and smashed. However, the damage inside the *Skate*'s pressure hull was minimal and within three days she made a successful surface run. Submerging the boat, it was decided, would not have been safe. Operation Crossroads, as the tests were labeled, demonstrated that nuclear weapons could damage or sink ships, but that ships could also survive nuclear attack. (U.S. Navy)

KEEP CLEAR
DANGER!
VERY RADIO-ACTIVE

The *Sennet* (SS-408) was the first U.S. submarine to operate in the Antarctic. She accompanied the third Antarctic expedition led by Rear Admiral Richard E. Byrd—Operation Highjump—from December 1946 to March 1947. However, she was not considered a suitable ship for ice operation, being too vulnerable to ice damage. Note that one of her periscopes is fully extended. (U.S. Navy)

mile of where the bomb was dropped. Several ships were sunk and many more damaged to varying degrees. The bomb sunk and damaged more ships than had ever before been damaged by a single explosion. But most of the ships, even those near the aim point, survived. Three weeks later the target ships were subjected to a second atomic detonation. This time the bomb was suspended beneath a landing craft to produce an underwater detonation. The submarines *Tuna* and *Apogon* were sunk in the tests and others were severely damaged.

The Bikini tests demonstrated that warships could survive the atomic bombs then available to the United States and which, it was assumed, would be produced in the future by other nations. Although later weapons would be much more potent, there was sufficient encouragement from the survival of so many Bikini test ships to allow planning for new postwar naval classes to continue.

Of course many persons, some in the Navy, believed strongly that only submarines could survive attacks from aircraft and guided missiles. The Germans had used primitive, bomber-launched guided missiles against Italian and Allied warships in the Mediterranean with considerable success, and the Japanese *kamikaze* or suicide planes had indicated the potential effectiveness of anti-ship weapons with advanced guidance systems. Only a submarine, it was predicted, would be immune to attacks from future weapons of this sort.

However, the Navy's leadership felt that surface fleets could be protected against air and missile attack through the use of improved radars, carrier-launched fighter planes, advanced anti-aircraft guns, and defensive guided missiles that were already under development. The surface fleets of the postwar Navy, with large aircraft carriers at their center, would be used to strike against hostile land targets, especially ports, ship-

*A kiloton is the equivalent of one thousand tons of TNT. Thus, a 20-KT weapon was the equivalent of 20,000 tons of TNT.

The Bremen-built Type XXI submarine U-3008 was extensively evaluated by the U.S. Navy after the war. Here she is at sea on July 25, 1947. The U-3008 was one of ten U-boats acquired by the Navy as war booty from the Germans. Note her rounded bow and absence of large deck guns. The streamlined conning tower was installed in the United States. Inside she had advanced propulsion machinery and batteries. These features were incorporated in subsequent U.S. submarines and the GUPPY conversion program. (U.S. Navy)

Fleet Admiral Chester W. Nimitz, the Chief of Naval Operations, and other senior officers examine the U-2513 in May 1946. After being used on trials, the U-2513 was sunk in weapons tests in 1951, while the U-3008 was scrapped in 1951. Both were carefully examined by American submariners and engineers. (U.S. Navy)

The *Odax* (SS-484) was the first GUPPY conversion, being streamlined and fitted with improved storage batteries to provide an underwater speed of 18.2 knots, nearly double that of her fleet-boat configuration. Note the very small "sail" structure; a single periscope was retained and no suitable snorkel was available when she was converted. (U.S. Navy)

The *U-2513* with an American crew on board. Note the standard Type XXI conning tower with twin 20-mm AA gun turrets fitted into the front and rear of the conning tower. These high-speed, quiet, deep-diving submarines, armed with six bow tubes and 23 advanced torpedoes, were the most advanced submarine built during World War II. (U.S. Navy)

yards, and naval air bases in the Soviet Union. The role of submarines was less clear. Surely some submarines would operate in direct support of such surface striking fleets, especially in the radar picket role.

During the Okinawa campaign of 1945 the U.S. Navy had sent out destroyers over the horizon from the carriers to detect approaching Japanese aircraft with their radar. This permitted the carriers to launch defensive fighters and take other precautions. Because pickets were subjected to severe air attacks, the concept was born of having submarines serve in the picket role. After detecting the enemy aircraft and sounding the warning, submarines could submerge to evade attack. For as long as they could remain on the surface they could direct friendly fighters to the approaching enemy planes.

Another new submarine role born from the war was submarine-versus-submarine. Actually, this tactic had been used in World War I, with the British building a special class of submarines to operate against German U-boats. During World War II a large number of submarines were sunk by other undersea craft. (All were sunk with the victims caught on the surface, with the lone exception of the U-864, sunk by HMS *Venturer* off Norway on February 9, 1945. On that occasion both submarines were submerged).

At the end of World War II the Soviet Union, which had always had a relatively large submarine force, had overrun eastern Germany, capturing many unfinished U-boats, submarine yards, and German engineers and scientists. The U.S. Navy's intelligence community predicted that with these German resources the USSR could build a massive undersea armada of advanced-technology submarines. These undersea craft could, in a future conflict, cut off Britain and Western Europe from reinforcements from the United States. Thus, antisubmarine warfare (ASW) was another immediate mission put forward for U.S. submarines after the war.

The United States had also obtained German submarines and material after the war.

TABLE 6. POSTWAR SUBMARINE CLASSES

Hull Numbers	Number Completed	Class	Launched	Displacement	Length Overall	Speed	Torpedo Tubes	Crew
SSK 1 to 3	3	K–1 (later Barracuda)	1951	765/1,000	196	13/10	2/2 21-in.	48
SST 1 to 2	2	T–1 (later Mackerel)	1953	250/310	133	10/10	1/0 21-in.	14
AGSS 555	1	Dolphin	1968	800/930	152	—/12+	1/0 Xmtl.[1]	31[2]
SS–563 to 568	6	Tang	1951–1952	1,615/2,100	269	16/16	6/2 21-in.	83
AGSS–569	1	Albacore	1953	1,218/1,400	204	25/33	nil	40
SSR–572 to 573	2	Sailfish	1955–1956	2,030/2,500	350	19½/14	6/0 21-in.	95
SS–576	1	Darter	1956	1,620/2,100	268	17/20+	6/2 21-in.	85
SS–580 to 582	3	Barbel	1958–1959	1,742/2,637	219	15/30	6/0 21-in.	75
—	1	X–1	1955	31½/36⅓	49½	15/12	nil	4[3]

1. An experimental torpedo tube was originally fitted; later removed.
2. Includes up to seven scientists.
3. Six men could be carried for short missions.

The *Cobbler* (SS-344) was a GUPPY II conversion, with a "stepped" sail structure. There were several GUPPY variations. The larger sail was required to accommodate a snorkel mast and second periscope. In this April 1952 view the *Cobbler*'s radar mast is extended. (U.S. Navy)

Fifty-two submarines were converted to various GUPPY configurations (with some going through more than one configuration). In addition, nineteen fleet submarines were modified under the "fleet snorkel" program, most having their deck guns removed, a streamlined sail structure installed, and a snorkel installed. They could be easily identified by their original, ship-like bows. (U.S. Navy)

The *Razorback* (SS-394), a GUPPY IIA, at high speed on the surface off Oahu in 1961. A variety of sonar domes appeared on U.S. submarines after World War II, with the *Razorback* having two forward of her stepped sail structure. (U.S. Navy)

Under the Allied agreements, ten German U-boats were transferred to American custody, including two of the 1,620-ton Type XXI high-speed craft. Type XXIs had streamlined underwater hulls, high capacity batteries, and other features to give them a submerged speed of some 17 knots for 60 to 80 minutes, and an endurance of up to 100 hours at slower speeds. They could dive underwater in only 20 seconds, and their operating depth was 850 feet—more than twice that of comparable U.S. submarines.

The Type XXIs and other German U-boats had also been fitted with the *schnorchel* or snorkel breathing tube. This device permitted air to be drawn in for diesel engines while the submarine was running at periscope depth. Thus, diesels could be used to charge batteries and propel the submarine while projecting only the snorkel head above the water, a much smaller target for ASW forces to detect than a surfaced submarine. (The Type XXI performance cited above was without snorkel, using only battery power.)

To counter the projected threats of the second half of the twentieth century, and to incorporate German and other advanced submarine technology, the U.S. Navy began a series of submarine programs after the war. Some of these, admittedly, simply sought to develop new roles to justify additional submarines, but in total they reflected an intensive and innovative effort to determine submarine roles and missions.

GUPPY Submarines. GUPPY, an acronym for Greater Underwater Propulsive Power, was a program to improve the underwater performance of U.S. fleet-type submarines. The submarines were streamlined, with all deck guns removed and their conning towers rebuilt; their ship-like bows were rounded; improved, smaller batteries were fitted; and in most units one of the diesels was removed (resulting in slower surface speeds). Some of the early GUPPY conversions also lost a periscope and some reload torpedoes. With these changes underwater speed was increased to 16 knots or a fraction more.

The first GUPPY craft were the *Odax* (SS-

The radar-picket submarine *Spinax*
(SSR-489) on the surface off the San
Francisco Naval Shipyard. Radar-
picket submarines were intended to
scout ahead of surface task forces, to
give early warning of hostile air
attacks and then control interceptors
until they were forced to dive to survive attacks against them. (U.S.
Navy)

There were several configurations of radar picket submarine conversions. This is the *Burrfish* (SSR-312) in the Mediterranean during the early 1950s. She has a modified fleet-boat conning tower with three large pylon structures for radar antennas. Two of her original six bow tubes and all four stern tubes have been removed, the latter to provide berthing for crewmen displaced by an air control center aft of the control room. (U.S. Navy)

484), and *Pomodon* (SS-486), converted in about six months each. Fifty more GUPPY craft followed, forty-five conversions plus five boats on which work had halted when the war ended; the *Tiru* (SS-416), *Volador* (SS-490), *Grampus* (SS-523), *Pickerel* (SS-524), and *Grenadier* (SS-525). The initial GUPPY design was improved upon, there being four major GUPPY configurations, with some boats being successfully upgraded to later configurations. These submarines were employed in first-line U.S. service into the 1970s.

Fleet Snorkel Submarines. While almost all of the GUPPY submarines were fitted with snorkels, a separate program was initiated to provide other fleet submarines with a snorkel and limited modernization. The high cost of GUPPY conversions had led to this program, and a number of boats received streamlined deck structures, snorkel, and other improvements. However, they retained the pointed bow and some continued to carry deck guns for short periods.

Radar Picket Submarines. Ten submarines were converted to the radar picket configuration. The first submarines modified for this role were the *Requin* (SS-481) and *Spinax* (SS-489), which were hastily fitted in 1946 with modified ship radars. After that, fleet boats were taken in hand for more extensive conversions. These submarines, redesignated SSR upon conversion, were fitted with air-search radars, the stern torpedo tubes (and bow tubes in two boats) were removed for additional crew berthing, and space was rearranged inside the submarine for electronic equipment and an air control center. As improved radars became available, it was deemed necessary to provide still more space. Six of the *Gato*-class submarines were cut in half forward of the conning tower and a 24-foot hull section was inserted.

The SSR conversion program was considered so successful that plans were drawn up for new-construction radar pickets. The *Sailfish* (SSR-572) and *Salmon* (SSR-573) were constructed in the early 1950s speci-

The *Raton* (SSR-270) shows a more advanced radar-picket configuration, with her hull lengthened, a streamlined sail built over her conning tower, and more capable radars. All six forward tubes were retained, but, again, the after tubes were deleted in her SSR conversion. This photo was taken in Tokyo Bay in 1955. (U.S. Navy)

The *Bass* (SSK-2), one of three small hunter-killer submarines, at sea in 1957. Note the huge sonar dome. The K-boats were relatively quiet and had the highly effective AN/BQR-4 array sonar; however, they were too small and too slow to be effective in the role envisioned for them. Seven fleet boats were converted to the SSK role with modified BQR-4 sonars. (U.S. Navy)

A rare view of an entire submarine division at sea, in this view Submarine Squadron 21 with the *Blenny* (SS-324), *Clamagore* (SS-343), *Cobbler* (SS-344), and *Corporal* (SS-346). The *Blenny* was a GUPPY IA and the others GUPPY IIs. Note the high plastic sail structures; three fin-like hydrophones for AN/BQG-4 PUFFS (Passive Underwater Fire Control). All war-built submarines have been stricken from the U.S. Navy, but many GUPPY-types remain in foreign service. (U.S. Navy)

The *Salmon* (SSR-573) was one of two large, built-for-the-purpose radar-picket submarines with conventional propulsion. She and her sister submarine *Sailfish* (SSR-572) had a limited career as pickets and operated as attack submarines (SS) from 1961 until stricken in 1977-78. (U. S. Navy)

The first of the small hunter-killer submarines, the *Barracuda* (SSK-1) at sea in November 1951. Note the huge bow sonar dome. The K-boats were relatively quiet and had the highly effective AN/BQR-4 array sonar; however, they were too small and too slow to be effective in the role envisioned for them. Seven fleet boats were converted to the SSK role with modified BQR-4 sonars. (U.S. Navy)

fically for this role. With a surface displacement of 2,615 tons and overall length of 350½ feet, they were the largest conventionally propelled submarines to be built by the United States, except for the *Argonaut* and N-boats of the 1930s.

And, to help justify the development of a two-reactor nuclear submarine, in 1956 the Navy laid the keel for the USS *Triton* (SSRN-586), which, at almost 6,000 tons standard displacement and 447½ feet in length, was a still larger radar picket submarine. Its career would be both brief and dramatic (see Chapter 7).

The radar picket concept was soon overtaken by advances in shipboard and aircraft radar and other electronic-warfare developments, and the SSRs were all discarded by the end of the 1950s.

Killer Submarines. The program to develop submarines specifically for the ASW role took two tracks: the construction of small hunter-killer submarines that could be mass-produced in wartime, and the conversion of larger fleet boats. The killer submarines were to lie in wait off Soviet ports and in narrow straits, ambushing enemy submarines going out to sea. The killer submarines would thus operate at shallow depths, at slow speed, for long periods of time. Large sonars would be fitted to detect the hostile boats; thus large bow sonar domes (with torpedo tubes in the conversions reduced) and advanced torpedo fire-control systems were required.

First came the built-for-the-purpose K-boats, the K-1, K-2, and K-3, completed in 1951–52.* (They were assigned hull numbers SSK-1 to -3). These were the smallest U.S. submarines built in more than three decades, with a surface displacement of only 765 tons and a length of 196 feet. A large AN/BQR-4 sonar filled the bows of the K-boats. This was a passive array sonar, derived from improvements to the German GHG sonar of the Type XXI U-boats.

The Navy planned to continue peacetime production of the K-boats to maintain the

---

*These submarines were later renamed *Barracuda*, *Bass*, and *Bonita* respectively.

The *Perch* (as SSP-313) in her
original transport configuration
shortly after her 1948 conversion at
Mare Island. She still has her gun
armament forward and the cargo
hangar aft. (U.S. Navy)

The *Bream* (SSK-243), one of the
seven large hunter-killer boats, off
Point Loma (San Diego), California.
Her bow houses an AN/BQR-4A
array sonar. Two bow tubes were removed and the boats were modified
to reduce self-generated noises.
But they were not GUPPY variants,
despite their appearance. (U.S.
Navy)

These Marine scouts leaving the *Sealion* (ASSP-315) in May 1956 are
from the 2nd Marine Division. Note
their HRS/H-19 helicopter resting on
the after deck; 5-inch/25-caliber and
40-mm guns are still carried. Shortly
after this photo was taken the *Sealion* was reclassified APSS-315. As
the LPSS-315 she was the last U.S.
war-built submarine in active U.S.
service, being decommissioned in
1970 and stricken in 1977. (U.S.
Navy)

The *Perch* (APSS-313) exercises with reconnaissance troops from the 1st Marine Division off the coast of California. In addition to many internal changes, the *Perch's* conning-tower structure had been extended and additional masts and shears added by January 1957, when this photo was taken. (U.S. Marine Corps)

Here the *Perch* is preparing to launch an LVT amphibious tractor during a 1949 exercise. The vehicle could be carried in the cargo hangar and launched by flooding down the submarine. (U.S. Navy)

capability of building hundreds in wartime. However, the original plan had been for the SSKs to be very small, up to 500 tons and 150 feet long; thus, they were much larger than planned. The SSKs were slow, as well as uncomfortable in the northern waters where they were to operate. Thus the program was halted after the first three boats, which were soon allocated to training and then weapon testing roles.

Seven of the larger *Gato*-class were converted to SSKs, being fitted with a modified BQR-4 sonar and special quieting features.

In addition to these killer-submarine developments, by the 1950s new torpedoes were available for the ASW role. The Mark 37 was a long-range torpedo that would travel straight for a preset distance and then run a preset pattern until the torpedo's acoustic guidance would detect a submarine. The torpedo would then "home" onto propeller noises of the enemy sub. Various models of the Mark 37 were developed, some with active/passive homing. In the active mode the torpedo sent out an acoustic signal to be reflected from an enemy submarine to guide the torpedo. The wire-guided Mark 37 provided the launching submarine with the ability to control the weapon through a thin wire that connected them early in the torpedo's run, making it possible to counter any movements by the enemy submarine that were detected by the U.S. submarine's sonar.

The killer-submarine concept of the 1950s was resurrected during the nuclear period, but in general the larger, more capable diesel and nuclear submarines could perform the killer mission as well as carrying out other submarine activities.

Cargo Submarines. After World War II the submarine *Barbero* (SS-317) was converted to a cargo submarine (being redesignated SSA and later as an auxiliary, ASSA). A number of U.S. and foreign submarines had carried cargo during the war, and the *Barbero* was modified to carry 28,300 gallons of fuel and 6,000 cubic feet (120 tons) of cargo. Two diesels and her stern tubes were re-

The *Grayback* (LPSS-574) as converted to a transport submarine. The twin missile hangars forward have been modified to carry small boats and swimmer delivery vehicles. The three fin-like domes are for AN/BQG-4 PUFFS. (U.S. Navy)

The *Mackerel* (SST-1) was one of two small training and target submarines built for the U.S. Navy. No further submarines of this type were built for the U.S. Navy, but in the late 1960s the Soviet Union built four larger Bravo-class submarines, apparently for this role. (U.S. Navy)

Prior to World War II several submarines were fitted to refuel seaplanes. During the war, this technique was extensively used by Germany and Japan, but not the United States. After the war the *Guavina* (SS-362) was modified to refuel seaplanes. Here she is topping off a P5M Marlin flying boat off Norfolk in 1955. At the time the *Guavina* was designated AGSS; she also carried the designations SSO and AOSS. The submarine tanker concept was not used operationally. (U. S. Navy)

Marines handle a rubber boat aboard the *Grayback*. The large hangar doors can be opened while the submarine is submerged to allow swimmers and delivery vehicles to float out. (U.S. Marine Corps)

These Marine reconnaissance specialists are on the *Grayback*'s sail, waiting for the submarine to surface fully. (U.S. Marine Corps)

moved and her internal arrangements were changed about. However, the project was considered of limited value and the *Barbero* was subsequently converted into a guided missile submarine.

Transport Submarines. The *Argonaut* and N-boats had been employed as commando transports in World War II, while other submarines carried raiding parties and frogmen on other missions. After the war the fleet boats *Perch* (SS-313) and *Sealion* (SS-315), were converted to transport submarines (initially SSP). All torpedo tubes and two diesel generators were removed, and special modifications were made to permit them to accommodate 111 troops and their equipment. A pressure cylinder was installed aft of the conning tower that could carry an LVT amphibious tractor, a jeep, or rubber rafts. Helicopters periodically landed aboard the transport submarines in exercises and the *Sealion* on one occasion submerged with a Bell H-13 helicopter in the cylinder/hangar.

Later, when the Navy phased out guided missile submarines, the former fleet boat *Tunny* (SS-282) was employed in this role during the 1960s. Two later built-for-the-purpose guided missile submarines, the *Grayback* (SSG-574) and *Growler* (SSG-577) were planned for conversion to transport submarines in the later 1960s. However, funding problems led to only the *Grayback* being converted. As the LPSS-575 her two missile hangars have been converted to hold swimmer transport vehicles and the 2,670-ton, 334-foot submarine had facilities for 67 troops.

The *Perch* was the only U.S. submarine to win a combat citation during the Korean War, being employed in September 1950 to carry British commandos in a raid on the northeast coast of Korea. The Royal Marines blew up a train tunnel on a key Communist supply line. The one man killed in the action was buried at sea from the *Perch*. During 1965-66 the *Perch* carried out landings in Vietnam and served as an underwater base for frogmen carrying out beach reconnaissance operations.

The *Grouper* was the first of the large SSK conversions; subsequently she became a sonar test platform for the Naval Underwater Sound Laboratory at New London, Connecticut. Shown here in that role as the AGSS-214, the *Grouper* has a number of sonar systems installed. (U. S. Navy)

The *Tigrone* (as AGSS-419) as a research platform for the Naval Underwater Sound Laboratory during the 1960s. Her bow has been rebuilt to accommodate experimental sound gear, and there is a test installation on her deck aft of the conning tower. Gone are all indications of her previous incarnation as an SSR. (U.S. Navy)

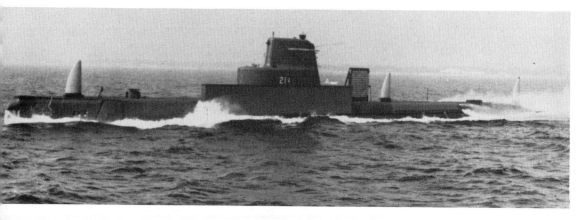

The *Flying Fish* (AGSS-229) was fitted with the large conformal array sonar from the German heavy cruiser *Prinz Eugen* (sunk at Bikini as a target ship with the U.S. designation IX-300). Known as GHG (for *Gruppen Hörsch Gerat*), the sonar was used in the cruiser for torpedo detection. A modified system was fitted in the Type XXI U-boats and evolved into the American AN/BQR-4. In this 1951 photo the *Flying Fish* rests at a pier with the fleet submarine *Sarda* (SS-488). The 229 was decommissioned in 1958. (Courtesy M.L. Hultgren and *General Dynamics News*)

The "revolutionary" *Albacore* (AGSS-569) provided the basis for subsequent U.S. nuclear submarine hull designs. Capable of better than 30-knot speeds underwater, the "tear drop" configuration was based on much earlier spindle-hull design concepts. In this view the *Albacore* has X-shaped tail planes, one of several modifications tested by the craft from her completion in early 1954 until she was laid up in reserve in 1972. (U.S. Navy)

The blunt-bow *Baya* (AGSS-318) underway as a sonar test submarine in 1962. The *Baya* was lengthened and her bow completely rebuilt to accommodate new sonar equipment. She had several configurations as a sonar research and test platform, including being fitted with the three hydrophone fins of the AN/BQG-4 PUFFS. (U.S. Navy, PH2 P.T. Skalski)

Minelaying Submarines. After the war the Navy also drew up plans to convert a fleet submarine to a minelayer (SSM), the first such specialized submarine since the *Argonaut* (SM-1/SS-166). The *Picuda* (SS-382) was tagged for the SSM role, but the project was dropped, influenced in part by the ability of all submarines to plant mines from their torpedo tubes.

Submarine Tanker. The interest shown during the 1930s and World War II in refueling seaplanes at forward locations from submarines was revived after the war with conversion of the fleet boat *Guavina* (SS-362) to a submarine oiler (SSO and later ASSO). She was fitted with side blisters (increasing her beam from 27 to 37 feet) and only two stern torpedo tubes were retained. Thus reconfigured, she could carry 160,000 gallons of fuel. She was used in trials to refuel seaplanes and it was intended that submarine tankers could be coupled with the P6M Seamaster, a jet-powered strike seaplane, to provide a very long attack range. However, the P6M project was cancelled in 1959. Tests with the *Guavina* included an underwater refueling of the submarine *Dogfish* (SS-350), the only known operation of that kind by any navy.

Training and Target Submarines. After World War II the U.S. Navy also looked into the feasibility of using small submarines to help train anti-submarine forces, especially in the hunting and killing of high-speed submarines. To provide this service for various U.S. ASW units, two small submarines—smaller than even the K-boats—were constructed after the war. These craft had a surface displacement of only 250 tons and were 133 feet in length. They had conventional diesel-electric propulsion, and only a single bow torpedo tube.

Like the K-boats, these craft initially had letter-number names, the T-1 and T-2, and started a new series of hull designations, SST-1 and SST-2, respectively. Both were completed in 1953 and were subsequently assigned fish names in 1956—the *Mackerel* (SST-1) and *Marlin* (SST-2)—carrying the

The *Albacore* in an earlier configuration displays a multi-tone paint scheme. Her bow planes, folded for surface running, and tail fin/rudder are visible in this photo. Tear-drop submarines travel faster submerged than on the surface. The *Albacore* was unarmed. This photo was taken in April 1954, shortly after her completion. (U. S. Navy)

The *Dolphin* (AGSS-555)—or "nickle boat"—in her original configuration as a deep-diving research submarine. When completed in 1968 she was the first U.S. non-nuclear submarine built in almost a decade. She has since been modified several times, as she has been employed as a research craft at depths greater than those at which American combat submarines can operate. (U.S. Navy)

The *Dolphin* in one of her later configurations with a dome for the AN/BQS-15 sonar. She was the last diesel-electric submarine constructed for the United States. (U.S. Navy)

The *Tang* (SS-563) was the first of seven conventional attack submarines built by the U.S. Navy after World War II with their design drawing heavily on the German Type XXI series. The U.S. submarines initially went to sea with a radical "pancake" diesel engine. Intended to reduce the space required for main engines, it suffered severe problems and the Navy replaced it with a more conventional diesel. Here the *Tang* is departing Pearl Harbor. (U.S. Navy, PHCS Robert A. Carlisle)

M-names borne by the two comparatively small submarines built by the Navy in the late 1930s. These T-boats performed valuable services during the 1950s and 1960s, being later joined by the K-boat *Barracuda*, which became the SST-3 in 1959.

Research and Auxiliary Submarines. A number of fleet boats have been modified to various degrees to perform research and auxiliary functions. Beginning in 1949, when the *Manta* (SS-299) was modified to serve as an underwater target, seven research submarines were changed to miscellaneous auxiliary (AGSS). The *Manta*'s conversion provided large blisters to absorb the hits by non-warhead homing torpedoes.

Subsequently, the *Baya* (SS-318), *Flying Fish* (SS-229), *Grouper* (SSK-214), and *Tigrone* (SSR-419) were modified for acoustic/sonar research, while the *Sea Cat* (SS-399) carried an AGSS designation from 1949 to 1952 while fitted with special equipment, and the *Archerfish* (SS-311) was converted to an oceanographic research craft. Some of these boats underwent several configuration changes. While an AGSS, on February 29, 1952, the *Flying Fish* made her 5,000th dive, the first American submarine to reach that mark. And the *Archerfish*, at times claiming an all-bachelor crew, made a circumnavigation of the world while carrying out her ocean survey activities.

Beyond the fleet submarine conversions to research roles, the Navy has constructed two specialized research submarines. The first was the *Albacore* (AGSS-569), completed in 1952 to test a high-speed hull form. For several decades U.S. submarines had outer hull forms intended primarily for high-speed surface operations. The *Albacore* hull form with a very low length-to-beam ratio (210½ feet long with a 27½-foot beam) was shaped more like a fat cigar or blimp than a traditional submarine. The streamlined hull had no wooden deck structure. With conventional diesel-electric propulsion, the *Albacore* could easily exceed 30 knots submerged and was rated as the world's fastest submarine at the time. She was unarmed and

This is a later photo of the *Tang*-class submarine *Gudgeon* (SS-567). She has been fitted with the three-fin AN/BQG-4 PUFFS. (U.S. Navy, PH3 J.B. Land)

The *Darter* (SS-576) is an improved *Tang*-class submarine, the only one of her design completed. This view shows her at high speed on the surface during operations in the Western Pacific. (Giorgio Arra)

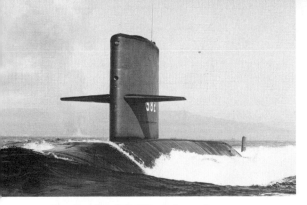

The *Bonefish* (SS-582) on the surface at high speed makes a striking picture, as she maneuvers off Oahu in 1966. Note that her diving planes have been moved from the bow to her sail structure, as in the later nuclear submarines. (U.S. Navy, PH1 D.J. Kosbiel)

The *Blueback* entering port with crewmen ready to handle lines. Her *Albacore*-type hull with wide beam and blunt bow is clearly visible. An improved *Barbel*-design submarine has been built by the Netherlands Navy. (Giorgio Arra)

The *Blueback* (SS-581) was one of three attack submarines built to the *Albacore* design with conventional propulsion. All three submarines of the *Barbel* (SS-580) class remained in active service into the early 1980s. Their submerged noise levels were quieter than those of nuclear submarines, thus affording them tactical advantages in exercises. (U.S. Navy)

underwent several changes in her configuration while employed in the test role.

The second built-for-the-purpose AGSS was the *Dolphin* (AGSS-555),* which was first commissioned in 1968. The *Dolphin* was designed specifically for deep-diving operations and at the time could operate deeper than any other military submarine. The craft has a 15-foot constant-diameter hull of advanced steel, capped at both ends. A single, experimental torpedo tube was fitted until 1970. The submarine has carried out a number of deep-ocean research missions in support of various Navy programs.

While these nine submarines carried the AGSS designation in the research role, at a later date a large number of fleet boats, many having carried other specialized designations, were changed to AGSS as an administrative measure so that they would not be "charged" against the Navy's attack-submarine force levels. Similarly, submarines used as immobilized dockside trainers by the Naval Reserve were changed to AGSS from 1962 onward, and the survivors to IXSS (for miscellaneous unclassified submarine) from 1971. The Naval Reserve submarine program ended in 1971, and the remaining boats were discarded or became memorials.

Midget Submarines. Britain, Italy, and Japan made extensive use of midget submarines during World War II. The United States, however, did not construct or operate any midgets. After the war the U.S. Navy conducted tests with a British X-craft and then constructed the only true American midget submarine, the X-1. Completed in 1955, she was to be the prototype for a series of such submarines that could penetrate enemy harbors in wartime. The X-1 had a surface displacement of 31½ tons, was 49½ feet long, and carried a crew of four. (Six men could be carried for shorter missions.) She had a lock-out chamber for swimmers who were to attach explosives to the hulls of enemy ships found at anchor.

The X-1 was originally fitted with a hy-

*The *Dolphin*'s hull number was taken from a block of numbers cancelled late in World War II.

The X-1 was the only midget submarine to be constructed for the U.S. Navy. The craft was built after U.S. evaluation of a British X-craft. After tests the midget-submarine concept was discarded by the Navy and the X-1 served as a test platform for various experiments, mostly in the Annapolis area, where the Navy has an engineering laboratory complex. (U.S. Navy)

After World War II a large number of submarines were transferred to foreign navies. This is the "semi-streamlined" Greek submarine *Poseidon*, formerly the USS *Lapon* (SS-260). She and the *Jack* (SS-259) were transferred to the Hellenic Navy in 1957-58. As the fleet boats and GUPPY types wore out, most foreign navies went to European sources for advanced diesel-electric submarines.

This photo and the preceding one of the X-1 were taken in November 1960 while the midget submarine was undergoing work at the Philadelphia Naval Shipyard (as the navy yards were redesignated after World War II). The X-1 had only stern control surfaces, with no bow planes. Note the small "conning tower" and the spray shield for the forward hatch. (U.S. Navy)

A squadron of submarines with crews at attention nest alongside the tender *Nereus* (AS-17) at San Diego during a change of command ceremony in August 1955. The submarines are the *Tunny* (SSG-282), *Cusk* (SS-348), *Carbonero* (SSG-337), *Tilefish* (SS-307), *Spinax* (SSR-489), *Rock* (SSR-274), *Remora* (SS-487), *Catfish* (SS-339), and *Volador* (SS-490). The submarine rescue vessel *Florikan* (ASR-9) is moored off the tender's bow. (U.S. Navy)

drogen-peroxide propulsion plant which permitted the operation of her diesel engine while submerged. A small electric motor was fitted for "creeping" speeds. A more conventional diesel-electric plant was fitted in the early 1960s after an accidental explosion of the volatile hydrogen peroxide blew the craft apart in 1958. After extensive tests and evaluation in 1956-57, the X-1 was laid up until 1960. She was then used in research projects until 1973.

Attack Boats. Postwar shipbuilding programs for the U.S. Navy began with the fiscal 1947 budget which included funds for the first new-construction fast attack submarines. The construction of attack submarines would continue on an annual basis despite the large effort allocated to special-purpose submarines.

The first American postwar attack submarines were the six *Tang*-class, with all carrying the names of boats lost in World War II combat. Originally displacing 1,600 tons on the surface and 262 feet in length, the *Tang* (SS-563) and her sister boats, plus the later *Darter* (SS-576), drew heavily on Type XXI technology and design features. However, innovative features included small, "pancake"-type diesel engines that proved most troublesome. They were soon replaced, with the boats being lengthened to 278 feet to accommodate their new power plants. Submerged speed for these postwar boats was some 17 knots.

After these seven *Tang*-design boats were constructed, the Navy adopted the *Albacore*-type hull, and the next three attack submarines were of the highly advanced *Barbel* (SS-580) class. Displacing 1,740 tons surfaced with length of only 219 feet, these boats could exceed 30 knots submerged and proved to be among the most successful diesel submarines yet built by any nation.

All three *Barbel*s were completed in 1959. By that time the USS *Nautilus* (SSN-571) had been at sea four years. The Navy sought no more conventionally powered attack submarines, instead pushing for only nuclear attack submarines—the SSNs.

Two fleet boats were used in most unusual activities after the war. The *Hake* (SS-256) was intentionally sunk and then raised in a 1969 salvage exercise off the Atlantic coast to evaluate new salvage techniques and train diving and salvage personnel. Here she wallows on the surface amidst pontoons; a floating dry dock is in the background. The *Toro* (SS-422) was zebra-striped and prepared for sinking after the nuclear submarine *Thresher* (SSN-593) was lost in 1963. It was hoped that by observing the fall of the *Toro*, the Navy scientists could better understand the movement of a submarine falling out of control through the depths. All wooden deck structure, cables, and other materials that might break loose were cut away. However, she was not used in the experiment and was later sold for scrapping. (U.S. Navy; *Hake* photo by Hal Stoelzle)

The GUPPY II submarine *Pickerel*
(SS-524) surfaces dramatically at a
48-degree angle from a depth of 150
feet off Oahu. (U.S. Navy)

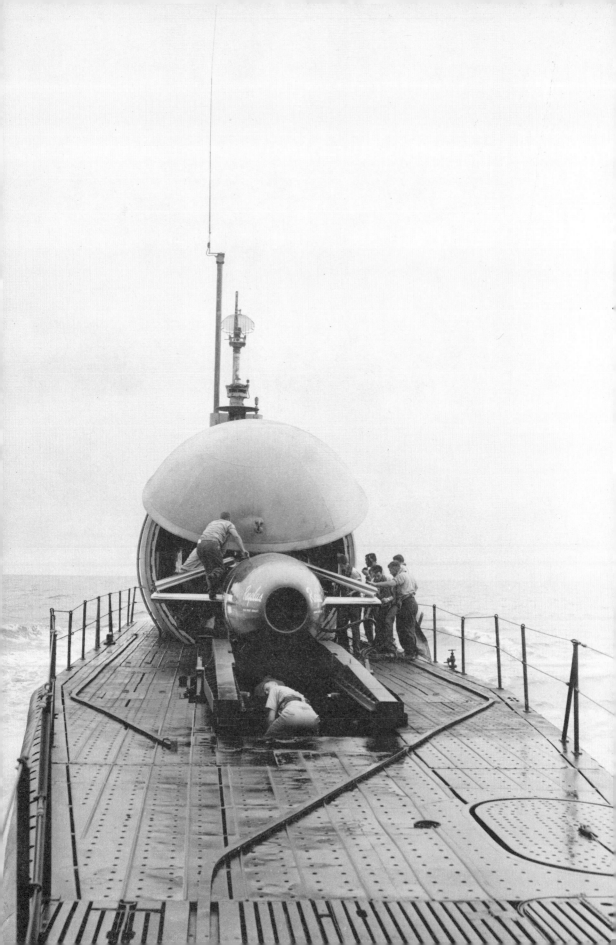

A Regulus missile is prepared for launching aboard the *Barbero*. Two missiles with wings folded could be accommodated in the hangar. This particular shot, on June 7, 1959, consisted of the missile being loaded with U.S. mail and flown ashore to be landed by radio control, as a demonstration of the potential of missiles for non-military uses. (U.S. Navy)

7. GUIDED MISSILE SUBMARINES

From the outset of its development the submarine was considered a "strategic" weapon; many saw it being used to blockade an enemy's coastlines, starve his population, and force surrender. German U-boats were used in this way in both World Wars, while U.S. submarines in the Pacific during 1942-45 helped to bring devastation to the Japanese homeland.

Still, submarines were "tactical" weapons in the same sense that they were used as naval weapons at sea. Admittedly, in World War II they did on occasion land agents or raiders on hostile beaches, and shell enemy coasts. Japanese submarines twice launched small floatplanes to bomb the American coast. But their ability to inflict major damage on enemy territory was virtually nil.

The German Army of the Third Reich appears to have first looked at the concept of firing missiles from submarines. During the war the submarine U-511 was experimentally fitted with six rocket-launching racks by engineers from the Peenemunde rocket research center. These were small, bombardment rockets. The U-511 moved out into the Baltic and, with her deck about twenty-five feet beneath the waves, successfully fired some two dozen of the four-foot rockets, which struck the surface some two miles away.

German Army-Navy interservice rivalry prevented continuation of the tests, although the German Navy later tried—unsuccessfully—to repeat the rocket-firing experiments. Then, in the closing stages of World War II a number of German V-1 "buzz bombs" fell into American hands. An air-breathing pulsejet engine could propel the 25-foot missile at 360 m.p.h. for about 150 miles (later boosted to 230 miles by the Germans). Preset guidance devices could send the V-1 diving on a fixed target with a 2,200-pound high-explosive warhead.

The U.S. Army and Navy immediately expressed interest in using V-1s to attack Japan in the final assaults of the war, planned for 1945-46. Although not employed by U.S.

The *Carbonero* (SS-337) in 1949 with a Loon test missile on a catapult being checked out in preparation for launching. The Loon was an Americanized version of the German V-1 buzz bomb. The *Carbonero* does not have a hangar to house the missile. She performed her missile experiments with an SS designation rather than SSG. (U.S. Navy)

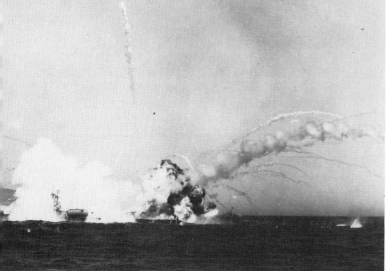

This Loon missile exploded during launch countdown on the deck of the *Cusk* (SSG-348) as the submarine was operating off Point Mugu, California. The decks had already been cleared for the launch and no personnel were topside. (U.S. Navy)

The *Barbero* (SSG-317), on the surface immediately before launching a Regulus I missile on a test firing in Hawaiian waters. The hangar is still ajar and a few men are on her deck and conning tower. Note the snorkel and radar masts aft of the periscope shears of this *Balao*-class submarine. (U.S. Navy)

A Loon test vehicle blasts off from the *Carbonero* during a series of 1949 flight tests from the submarine. The similar *Cusk* (SSG-348) was eventually fitted with a hangar. (U.S. Navy)

The Regulus I was the first U.S. strategic missile to be deployed. The turbojet-powered missile was operationally deployed aboard surface warships and submarines in the Western Pacific from the late 1950s until 1964, when Polaris became available in large numbers. The "Reg" could deliver a nuclear warhead against targets some 500 miles from the launching ship. Here a chase plane banks in preparation for accompanying the flight of this test missile. (U.S. Navy)

forces, the V-1 was extensively tested by the American services and an Americanized version known as the Loon was produced. The U.S. Navy modified the fleet submarine *Cusk* (SS-348) with a ramp for launching the Loon, and on February 12, 1947, she launched the first guided missile to be fired from a submarine. More shots followed and the fleet boat *Carbonero* (SS-337) was similarly modified.

With the Loon project providing technical data on missile launchings, the U.S. Navy started several submarine missile programs. The plan was to develop a weapon that the submarine could carry in a watertight hangar and surface to launch against a land target. The successful product of this effort was the Regulus I, which made its first flight test in 1950.

The Regulus I was essentially an unmanned aircraft, resembling a swept-wing jet fighter some 33 feet long. The missile could fly at some 600 m.p.h. for 500 miles and deliver a nuclear warhead against a fixed target. The missile could be preset to following a number of flight profiles. For example, it could fly most of the way to the target at perhaps 35,000 feet, drop to 600 feet when 50 miles from the target to help evade detection, and then power dive onto the target.

In the mid-1950s the fleet boats *Tunny* and *Barbero* were converted to Regulus craft (designated SSG-282 and SSG-317, respectively). These submarines were provided with missile checkout equipment, the associated electronic equipment, and provisions for arming the nuclear warheads. Aft of their conning tower a hangar was installed that could hold two Regulus missiles with their wings folded. To fire their "birds," the submarines would surface, prepare the launching ramp, extract a missile from the hangar, load it on the ramp, spread its wings, and, after checkout, fire.

The potential effectiveness of the Regulus submarine strike system led to a new construction program for missile submarines. The large *Grayback* (SSG-574) displaced 3,600 tons surfaced and was 322 feet long. With the similar *Growler* (SSG-577) she was

TABLE 7. GUIDED MISSILE SUBMARINES

Hull Number	Name	Launched	Converted	Displacement	Length Overall	Speed	Torpedo Tubes	Regulus Missiles[1]	Crew
SSG–282	*Tunny*	1942	1952	1,525/2,400	312	17/9	6/4 21-in.	2	85
SSG–317	*Barbero*	1943	1955	1,525/2,410	312	14/9	6/0 21-in.	2	85
SS–337[2]	*Carbonero*	1944	1949	1,525/2,400	312	17/8	6/4 21-in.	(Loon)	85
SSG–348	*Cusk*	1945	1948	1,525/2,400	312	17/8	6/4 21-in.	(Loon)	85
SSG–574	*Grayback*	1957	—	2,670/3,650	334	20/12	6/2 21-in.	$\frac{4}{2}$	95
SSG–577	*Growler*	1957	—	2,450/3,515	317½	20/12	4/2 21-in.	$\frac{4}{2}$	95
SSGN–586	*Halibut*	1959	—	3,850/5,000	350	15½/15	4/2 21-in.	$\frac{5}{2}$	120
SSGN–594[3]	*Permit*	—	—	3,500/4,000+	360	—/—	—	$\frac{0}{4}$	—

1. Regulus I missiles in *Tunny* and *Barbero*; Regulus I over Regulus II capacity in later submarines.
2. The *Carbonero* was not reclassified as SSG.
3. These submarines were completed as attack craft (SSN) of the *Thresher* class (SSN-593).

The *Grayback* launches the Regulus II missile in a blast of flame and smoke from the booster rockets. This weapon, which was to have been capable of delivering a nuclear warhead at supersonic speeds to targets 1,000 miles away, was cancelled in favor of the Polaris and because of Navy funding problems. The 11-ton weapon was intended to have a secondary anti-ship role. (Chance Vought Aircraft)

The landing ship *King County* (LST-857) was fitted with a submarine hangar and launching system to evaluate the Regulus II missile. Shown here in 1958 as the experimental ship AG-157, she has a Regulus II being readied for launch. The structure behind the missile is a non-submarine blast shield to protect the ship's superstructure. (U.S. Navy)

There was only one submarine firing of the Regulus II missile. This is a bow-on view of the *Grayback* during preparations for that shot. The missile is on the launching ramp, but the submarine's port hangar door is still raised. (U.S. Navy)

The Regulus missile submarines *Grayback* (left) and *Growler* were similar in design, but were not sisterships, as evidenced in this 1964 photograph showing the two craft at the Mare Island Naval Shipyard. A Navy censor has marked out an antenna above the *Growler*'s sail structure. (U.S. Navy)

completed in 1958. Both submarines had torpedo tubes, but their main feature was a pair of hangars faired into their bows. Each hangar could accommodate two Regulus I missiles or one of the improved Regulus II missiles.

The later missile was larger, capable of supersonic speeds and striking targets some 1,000 miles away from the launching submarine. The Regulus II was first flown in late 1957 and on September 16, 1958, the *Grayback* successfully fired one of the 11-ton missiles while operating off the California coast. She was the first and only submarine to fire the Regulus II. Three months later the Regulus production program was halted as the Navy shifted its emphasis to the Polaris ballistic missile.

Already under construction when the Regulus II was cancelled was the USS *Halibut* (SSGN-587), a nuclear-propelled missile submarine. The *Halibut* had been planned as a conventional submarine, but as she was being started the decision was made to give her nuclear propulsion. Thus she emerged from the Mare Island Naval Shipyard in 1960 as a 3,845-ton, 350-foot guided missile submarine. Forward the *Halibut* had a large hangar 90 feet long that was intended to accommodate three Regulus II missiles, but could hold five of the smaller Regulus birds.

Several more advanced Regulus submarines were in the planning stages. These underwater missile ships were to have had four seperate hangars for Regulus II missiles. With the Regulus II cancellation they were immediately reordered as torpedo attack submarines of the *Thresher* class.

Thus, by early 1960 the Navy had five submarines that could carry and launch the Regulus I missile: the *Tunny* and *Barbero* (two each), the *Grayback* and *Growler* (four each), and the *Halibut* (five). From the late 1950s until 1964 the Navy operated one or two of these submarines on continuous patrol in the western Pacific, with a total of four or more missiles prepared for launching against targets in Soviet Siberia.*

*Several U.S. Navy aircraft carriers and cruisers were also fitted to fire the Regulus I missile.

Unlike Polaris and other ballistic missiles, the air-breathing Regulus missile was fired from the surface. This is a periscope's view of the *Grayback* surfacing and launching a Regulus I. The total surface-to-launch sequence was about eight minutes. (U.S. Navy)

A Regulus I missile blasts off from the *Halibut* during a test firing in the Hawaiian area. Rocket boosters launch the "bird" together with the turbojet engine. The *Halibut* was designed to carry two Regulus II missiles, but deployed with up to five Reg Is in her large hangar.(U.S. Navy)

The *Grayback* (SSG-574) was the first U.S. submarine to be constructed specifically for launching missiles. Here she is entering San Diego with a Regulus I missile on the launching ramp. Note the two large hangars faired into the bow. (U.S. Navy)

The *Halibut* (SSGN-587) was the only nuclear-propelled submarine built for the U.S. Navy that was designed specifically to launch guided missiles. Forward of her sail structure the missile-launching ramp is folded down almost flush with the deck; her missile hangar is faired into the bow, with a single door, the "hump" near the bow." (U.S. Navy)

The ultimate Regulus submarine: this underwater giant would have carried four Regulus II missiles in separate hangars. However, with the cancellation of the Regulus II program the SSGN program also stopped and the submarines authorized for this class were built as *Thresher*-class attack submarines. (U.S. Navy)

This Regulus deterrent program came to an end in 1964 as the Navy deployed Polaris submarines into the Pacific for the first time. The five Regulus missile submarines were then stripped of their missile-firing equipment. The *Tunny* and *Barbero* were soon discarded. The *Grayback* and *Growler* were decommissioned, with the former later being converted to a transport submarine (LPSS-574). The *Halibut* found employment in a research role for many years, although for political reasons she was given an SSN designation and not classified as an auxiliary submarine (i.e., AGSSN).

Interestingly, from 1964 until the late 1970s the U.S. Navy did not have guided missiles aboard submarines. Then, in response to the Soviet advances in surface warships, the Harpoon anti-ship missile was developed for launching from torpedo tubes and after that the longer-range Tomahawk missile. The Soviet Navy, which developed a large, submarine-launched guided or "cruise" missile almost at the same time as the Regulus, has continued that weapon in service. Known as the Shaddock (SS-N-3 and later SS-N-12), that weapon continues in operational use, although now apparently intended for use against Western warships and not land attack.

For the U.S. Navy, the Regulus program initiated the submarine into the strategic strike role.

A later view of the *Nautilus*, at sea in the 1970s after a major overhaul. She was decommissioned in 1980 in preparation for being preserved as a memorial ("historic relic"). (General Dynamics/Electric Boat)

8. THE EARLY NUCLEAR SUBMARINES

The U.S. Navy began preliminary research into nuclear propulsion for submarines in 1939, even before the so-called Einstein letter to President Roosevelt recommending that the United States undertake the development of nuclear weapons. Once the atomic bomb project began—the Manhattan Project—all fissionable materials were diverted to that effort and the small Navy program stopped. However, even before the war was over, the head of the Manhattan Project, General Leslie Groves, formed a committee to look into postwar uses of atomic energy. Nuclear ship propulsion was the principal recommendation.

Thus, after the war the Navy sent a contingent of naval officers and engineers to Oak Ridge, Tennessee, the center of American nuclear research. The senior naval officer in the group was an outspoken captain who had gained a reputation during the war as head of the electrical branch of the Bureau of Ships, Hyman G. Rickover. The Oak Ridge team, spurred on by the postwar Chief of the Bureau of Ships, Vice Admiral Earle Mills, and others in the Navy, soon embarked on developing a submarine nuclear reactor plant.

A nuclear reactor produces heat through the fission of uranium atoms. This fission consumes very small amounts of uranium. There is no combustion and hence no air is required—the perfect propulsion scheme for a submarine. The heat from the reactor is carried by the primary coolant (pressurized water in most submarines) to a steam generator. The water in this primary loop is radioactive from passing through the reactor. Within the steam generator the heat is transferred to the secondary system, creating steam which then drives turbines to turn the submarine's propeller shafts. In transferring the reactor's heat to the steam generator, the pressurized water is cooled and in turn cools down the reactor core while "picking up" heat for another cycle.

The Navy was actually dependent upon the Atomic Energy Commission, established

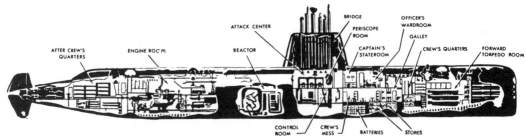

Cutaway drawing of the *Nautilus*
(U.S. Navy)

The *Nautilus* was the world's first
nuclear-propelled vehicle. She had a
conventional design, except for her
revolutionary power plant. Note the
folded bow planes and periscope
partially extended from large sail
structure. (U.S. Navy)

Welcome home! The *Nautilus* arrives
in New York City on August 25,
1958, after her historic voyage to the
top of the world. After mooring at
the naval shipyard in Brooklyn, her
crew was treated to a ticker-tape pa-
rade and other festivities. (U.S. Navy)

The central figure in the development of U.S. nuclear-propelled submarines has been Admiral Hyman G. Rickover. Originally appointed as the Navy's liaison to the Atomic Energy Commission when that agency was not moving fast enough to support Navy plans for nuclear ships, Rickover subsequently took complete control of nuclear submarine development. This photo shows him, typically, in civilian clothes aboard the *Nautilus* (SSN-571) in the 1950s. (U.S. Navy)

in January 1947, for development of the reactor plant. When the newly formed AEC delayed commitments, Admiral Mills made Rickover his liaison to the Commission. The feisty captain pushed, shoved, and drove the AEC and then the Navy into accelerating the nuclear submarine effort. In August 1951 the Navy awarded a contract to the Electric Boat Company to construct the world's first nuclear submarine, the *Nautilus* (SSN-571). The keel of the *Nautilus* was laid down at the EB yard in Groton, Connecticut, on Flag Day—June 14—1952. President Harry S. Truman spoke at the ceremonies, declaring: "The *Nautilus* will be able to move under water at a speed of more than twenty knots. A few ounces of uranium will give her ample fuel to travel thousands of miles at top speed. She will be able to stay under water indefinitely. Her atomic engine will permit her to be completely free of the earth's atmosphere. She will not even require a breathing tube [snorkel] to the surface."

A month later the Navy signed a contract with Electric Boat to construct a second nuclear-propelled submarine, the USS *Seawolf* (SSN-575). This submarine would use a liquid metal (sodium) to transfer heat from the reactor to the steam generator.

At the same time, the Navy and Atomic Energy Commission began constructing prototypes of the *Nautilus* and *Seawolf* plants at land sites in Arco, Idaho, and West Milton, New York, respectively. These reactors, which duplicated the reactor and steam plants for the submarines, would serve as training and research facilities.

The *Nautilus* was launched on January 21, 1954, with the wife of President Eisenhower smashing the traditional champagne bottle against her bow. The *Nautilus*, with a surface displacement of 3,530 tons and an overall length of 320 feet, was larger than the previous attack submarines, but conventional in design—except for her remarkable propulsion plant. The *Nautilus* got underway just after 11 A.M. on January 17, 1955, with the historic message UNDERWAY ON NUCLEAR POWER being signaled for the first time in history.

TABLE 8. EARLY NUCLEAR-POWERED SUBMARINES

Hull Numbers	Number Built	Class	Launched	Displacement	Length Overall	Speed	Torpedo Tubes	Crew
SSN–571	1	*Nautilus*	1954	3,530/4,090	320	18/20+	6/0 21-in.	110
SSN–575	1	*Seawolf*	1955	3,720/4,287	338	19/20+	6/0 21-in.	105
SSN–578 to 579 / SSN–583 to 584	4	*Skate*	1957–1958	2,555/2,850	268	15½/20+	6/2 21-in.	95
SSN–585	6	*Skipjack*	1958–1960	3,070/3,500	252	20/30+	6/0 21-in.	95
SSRN–586	1	*Triton*	1958	5,950/7,780	447½	27/20+	4/0 21-in.	172

The *Skate* (SSN-578) was the first U.S. nuclear submarine with a design suitable for series production. She was beaten out by the *Nautilus* as the first submarine to reach the North Pole, but she was the first undersea craft to surface through the ice at the top of the world. Arctic operations have become commonplace for U.S. and Soviet nuclear submarines. (U.S. Navy)

Modern submarines bring an unprecedented level of habitability to their crews. Nuclear power provides unlimited electricity for air conditioning and other purposes. This is the crew's mess of the *Nautilus*. It is also used for movies, briefings, and, as shown here between meals, as a lounge for off-duty sailors. (U.S. Navy)

The *Seawolf* at rest. No longer a first-line submarine, she is employed as a research vessel. The white markings on her sail structure are to help underwater mating operations with submersibles. (William Whalen, Jr.)

The giant radar picket submarine *Triton* (SSRN-586) on the surface at high speed. Note the large sail, with recessed AN/SPS-26 air-search radar antenna. She was the largest submarine built until that time, but her size and around-the-world cruise were overshadowed by the Polaris program. (General Electric)

Several short trials off the Atlantic coast followed to test the atomic sub. In May the *Nautilus* made her "shakedown" cruise from New London to San Juan, Puerto Rico. The cruise was made entirely submerged, 1,381 miles in 90 hours. The trip established several records. The distance was greater by a factor of ten than that previously traveled by a submarine without using a snorkel; it was the first time a combat submarine had maintained such a high submerged speed—an average of 16 knots—for more than an hour; it was the longest period an American submarine had remained underwater; and it was the fastest long-distance run by a submarine either on the surface or submerged. Later the *Nautilus* made an even faster passage, from Key West, Florida, to New London, a distance of 1,397 miles, at an average underwater speed of 20 knots. Although the Navy would say only that the *Nautilus* (and later submarines) could make more than 20 knots submerged, the pioneer atomic submarine had a maximum speed of about 23 knots.

More trials followed for the *Nautilus* and then operations with the fleet. In April of 1957, after more than two years of operation, the *Nautilus* had her uranium fuel core replaced. The submarine had steamed 62,562 miles, more than half of that distance submerged. During that period a conventional submarine with equal horsepower would have burned over two million gallons of diesel oil, enough to fill a two-mile-long train of 217 railroad tank cars. But more important was the submarine's submerged high-speed endurance which no conventional submarine could match.

The *Nautilus*'s second reactor core drove her for 91,324 miles, and her third for approximately 150,000 miles. Later nuclear cores can propel advanced nuclear submarines for some 400,000 miles, more than ten years of operation without refueling.

While the *Nautilus* was eminently successful, the second nuclear submarine, the *Seawolf*, encountered problems with her more complex sodium-cooled reactor plant. Sodium is highly corrosive and the *Seawolf* plant suffered major problems, the sub-

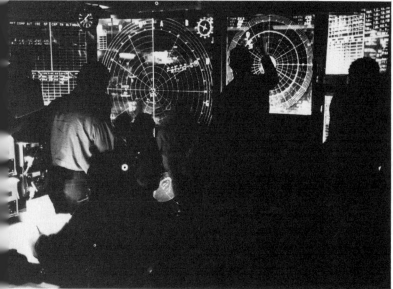

The first two nuclear submarines underway from their birthplace of Groton, Connecticut, en route to Long Island Sound. The *Seawolf* (SSN-575), foreground, has a different bow and sail configuration than the *Nautilus*. More significant, her liquid-sodium nuclear plant offered the potential of higher performance than the pressurized-water plant in the *Nautilus*. But problems plagued the *Seawolf* plant and she was later refitted with a *Nautilus*-type plant. (U.S. Navy)

This was the Combat Information Center (CIC) of the *Triton*, where men would track enemy aircraft and directly friendly fighters. But the *Triton* was never used operationally in the radar picket role. The SSR/SSRN concept was already being phased out by the time she was completed. (U.S. Navy)

The *Sargo* (SSN-583) of the *Skate* class was a pioneer in Arctic operations. She was the first nuclear submarine to be constructed at the Mare Island Naval Shipyard. Consideration is being given to again constructing nuclear subs at Mare Island to ease the problems at Newport News and Electric Boat. (Giorgio Arra)

The *Tullibee* (SSN-597) was a small hunter-killer submarine. Although extremely quiet with her nuclear-electric power plant, she was considered too small for many missions required of submarines. No additional submarines of this type have been built. The officers on the bridge give some indication of her small size. (General Dynamics/Electric Boat)

marine never achieving full horsepower or speed. However, even with her limitations, the *Seawolf* did exercise with the fleet and, in a test of underwater endurance of nuclear submarine crews, remained fully submerged for 30 consecutive days in 1958* and then for 60 consecutive days later in the year.

But the *Nautilus* made more impressive accomplishments when, in the summer of 1957, she began probes under the arctic ice pack. These were limited by equipment, under-ice experience, and military commitments. The initial probes were followed in 1958 by major efforts by the *Nautilus* to enter the ice pack between Alaska and Siberia, steam north to the top of the world, and then exit from the ice pack into the North Atlantic.

The early efforts to undertake such a trip were unsuccessful because of ice conditions. Finally, on July 23, 1958, the *Nautilus* glided out of Pearl Harbor and steamed northward. She successfully penetrated under the arctic ice and at 11:15 P.M. (Washington time) on August 3 the *Nautilus* crossed the North Pole. The pioneer atomic submarine was the first ship in history to reach the "top of the world." And, with fourteen officers, ninety-eight enlisted men, and four civilians on board, she brought more men to the North Pole than had ever before been assembled there.

The submarine then steamed south again, entering the open ocean between Greenland and Iceland. Her skipper, Commander William R. Anderson, was lifted from the deck of the *Nautilus* by helicopter, landed at a nearby air base, and flown to Washington for award ceremonies at the White House. Anderson was then flown across the Atlantic to England, and helicoptered out to the *Nautilus* just before the submarine entered Portsmouth for a tumultuous welcome.

The *Nautilus* thus pioneered not only nuclear propulsion but arctic transits by submarines, opening a new area for naval opera-

*The 30-day record was bettered about the same time by the USS *Skate* (SSN-578) which remained underwater for 53½ hours longer.

The *Nautilus* loads torpedoes at New London on December 19, 1955. The *Nautilus*, like other early nuclear submarines, had bow torpedo tubes; some of the other early classes also had stern tubes. (U.S. Navy)

Iceboats: the *Seadragon* (SSN-584), foreground, and her sister submarine *Skate* during a rendezvous at the North Pole in August 1962. Submarine operations in the polar area have both military and scientific missions. Note the men on the ice beyond the submarines. (U.S. Navy)

Sailors from the submarine *Seadragon* were clowning around on the ice during the craft's August 1960 arctic operation. This batter is ready for the first baseball ever pitched at the North Pole. (U.S. Navy)

The *Skipjack*-class submarines combined the tear-drop hull with nuclear propulsion. The *Scamp* (SSN-588) in Hong Kong harbor shows off the almost blimp-like lines of the class. Note the limited deck area, tall sail, and wing-like diving planes. (Giorgio Arra)

tions. Many nuclear submarines—American and Soviet—have followed her under the ice, but the *Nautilus* was first.

Meanwhile, the unsuccessful sodium-cooled plant was removed from the *Seawolf* and replaced by a pressurized-water plant similar to that of the *Nautilus*. This contributed to Admiral Rickover's decision to develop improved pressurized-water plants for all future U.S. nuclear submarines, each in large part an improvement of the previous one. The experimental—but torpedo-armed and fully equipped—*Nautilus* and *Seawolf* were followed by the four "production" submarines of the *Skate* (SSN-578) class. Also undertaken at this time were a number of specialized submarines, as the Navy sought to justify the development of improved nuclear submarine designs. These were the previously discussed radar picket submarine *Triton* (SSRN-586), with two nuclear reactors; the *Halibut* (SSGN-587) with Regulus missiles; and the small *Tullibee* (SSN-597), another attempt at a small, specialized hunter-killer submarine.

The *Nautilus*'s initial arctic transits were soon followed by those of other nuclear submarines, as the Navy sought to open the northern latitudes for potential military operations. The *Skate* was the second A-sub involved in arctic operations. Completed in late 1957, the *Skate* operated under arctic ice for ten days in mid-1958, traveling some 2,400 miles beneath the ice covering. She became the second ship in history to reach the North Pole. The following year she returned for special operations and on March 17, 1959, became the first submarine to surface through the ice at the geographic North Pole.

More under-ice operations by nuclear submarines followed. During 1960 the *Seadragon* (SSN-584) transited the fabled Northwest Passage, entering through Baffin Bay, between Baffin Island and Greenland. The *Seadragon* then steamed submerged through the Canadian archipelago. After reaching the Beaufort Sea the *Seadragon* turned toward the North Pole, which the submarine reached and surfaced at on August

The *Skipjack* at sea on trials in 1959. At the time she was the world's most advanced submarine. (U.S. Navy)

The *Sculpin* at high speed on the surface appears submerged. The *Skipjack*s were the U.S. Navy's fastest submarines upon completion. The subsequent classes were slower until the completion of the *Los Angeles* (SSN-688) in late 1976. (U.S. Navy)

25. When she returned to Pearl Harbor on September 14 the *Seadragon* had steamed 11,231 miles since leaving port, of which 10,415 were submerged and much of that under ice.

In mid-1962 the *Seadragon* returned to conduct joint under-ice operations with the *Skate*. Several other American nuclear submarines have travelled to the top of the world, and in 1962 a Soviet nuclear submarine, the *Leninsky Komsomol*, reached the North Pole—four years after the *Nautilus*'s historic cruise.

Other U.S. nuclear submarines made other cruises that were truly remarkable, including that of the *Triton*. Soon after her commissioning in November 1959, the *Triton*'s commanding officer, Edward L. Beach, was called to Washington and asked if the *Triton* could go around the world—submerged. Beach replied that she could and two weeks later, on February 16, 1960, the giant submarine slipped out to sea. Following much the same route taken by Ferdinand Magellan in 1519, the *Triton* steamed south into the Atlantic, rounded Cape Horn into the Pacific Ocean, across to Magellan Bay in the Philippines, then south through Lombok Strait, across the Indian Ocean, around the Cape of Good Hope, up to the coast of Spain, and then back across the Atlantic to the United States. The *Triton* surfaced off the coast of Deleware on May 10, 1960, having steamed 36,000 miles in 83 days and 10 hours since leaving the United States. Only twice had the *Triton* come briefly to the surface, once to take off an ill sailor, and once to take off a Navy information officer with films of the cruise. Both times the submarine merely broached her tall sail structure up out of the water and the man was transferred to a small boat sent over from a U.S. warship.

The *Triton*'s voyage had political significance, as President Eisenhower had hoped to use the cruise as another example of American technological superiority in the Cold War. As the *Triton* surfaced off the coast a helicopter plucked Beach from her deck and deposited him on the south lawn of the White House, where he was congratulated by the President. But ten days earlier an American U-2 spy plane had been shot down over the Soviet Union, and the achievements of the *Triton* were buried behind the international headlines of the day.

Similarly, the *Triton*'s potential place in the record of submarine development was denied. The radar picket mission was discarded by the U.S. Navy, and the technological achievements of the Polaris program overshadowed the *Triton*'s place as the only two-reactor submarine ever constructed.

In the late 1950s nuclear propulsion was "married" to the high-speed *Albacore* hull design in the *Skipjack* (SSN-585), completed in early 1959. The *Skipjack*, like the *Barbel*-class diesel submarines, was a comparatively small craft, displacing 3,070 tons on the surface and only 252 feet in length. However, her improved reactor plant, designated S5W, and tear-drop shape gave her a virtually unlimited underwater endurance at speeds of more than 30 knots.

Six *Skipjack*-class submarines were completed between 1959 and 1961. One, the USS *Scorpion* (SSN-589), was laid down twice. The original keel was placed on the building way at the Electric Boat yard on November 1, 1957. Two months later, on December 31, the then-unnamed SSN-589 was reordered as the Navy's first Polaris ballistic missile submarine, and another keel was laid down for the SSN-589.

Sailors aboard the *Triton* play chess
and snack as the submarine cruises
under the Pacific Ocean during her
circumnavigation. Food aboard
U.S. submarines is traditionally
very good. (U.S. Navy)

The *Triton* at sea. Intended to prove
both the feasibility of a multiple-
reactor nuclear plant and a large
radar picket submarine, she was
overtaken by events and technology.
(U.S. Navy)

Capt. Edward L. Beach, the commanding officer of the *Triton*, is lifted off by helicopter to be flown to the White House after the submarine's historic circumnavigation. (U.S. Navy)

The Polaris submarine *Sam Rayburn*
(SSBN-635) waits with all sixteen
missile tubes open. The firing rate
for these submarines is about one
missile every fifteen seconds. (U.S.
Navy)

9. THE POLARIS SUBMARINE

The first ballistic missile to be used in warfare was the V-2, which the Germans unleashed against England in September 1944. The 12-ton, 46-foot missile reached a speed of 3,000 m.p.h. as it fell, glowing hot, to earth with a one-ton warhead of high explosives. The Germans also designed a cannister in which a V-2 could be towed submerged behind a U-boat and then launched while at sea—against the United States. None of these was tested before the war ended.

A ballistic missile such as the V-2, unlike a guided or cruise missile, is not normally guided during flight. Rather, it is launched with a rocket engine providing thrust. During its climb the rocket propellant is exhausted and the missile continues skyward on a ballistic trajectory. After reaching its maximum altitude the missile turns downward and follows the ballistic flight path to its target. A ballistic missile's characteristics give it a very high speed and make it immune to all conventional modes of interception.

After the war U.S. Navy ordnance experts began to consider the feasibility of launching V-2s from surface ships and possibly even submarines. One V-2 was fired from the aircraft carrier *Midway*. As the missile lifted from the flight deck it veered to the side and their was some danger that it would strike the carrier's island superstructure. Also dangerous were the volatile missile fuels, with the V-2 using alcohol and liquid oxygen, the latter kept below *minus* 297° Farenheit.

Building on German technology and with German scientists brought to America after the war, the U.S. Army and Air Force embarked on major ballistic-missile programs. The Air Force believed that manned bombers were still the premier strategic striking force for the foreseeable future and that missiles were, at best, a supplemental means of delivering nuclear warheads. Indeed, Air Force emphasis at the time was on air-breathing, turbojet weapons rather than ballistic missiles.

In 1954 the Soviet Union exploded a fusion (hydrogen) bomb, just two years after the

TABLE 9. BALLISTIC MISSILE SUBMARINES

Hull Numbers	Number Built	Class	Launched	Displacement	Length Overall	Speed	Torpedo Tubes	Crew[1]
SSBN–598 to 602	5	*George Washington*	1959–1960	5,900/6,700	381⅔	~20/~25	6/0 21-in.	135
SSBN–608 to 611 } SSBN–618	5	*Ethan Allen*	1960–1962	6,900/7,900	410½	~20/~25	4/0 21-in.	135
SSBN–616 to 617 } SSBN–619 to 620 } SSBN–622 to 636	19	*Lafayette*	1962–1964	7,250/8,250	425	~20/~25	4/0 21-in.	135
SSBN–640 to 645 } SSBN–654 to 659	12	*Benjamin Franklin*[2]	1964–1966	7,250/8,250	425	~20/~25	4/0 21-in.	135

1. Two complete crews are assigned to each submarine.
2. Modified *Lafayette*-class submarines with quieter machinery.

Rear Admiral William F. (Red) Raborn—the man behind the Polaris program—chats with an officer and sailor aboard the Polaris submarine *George Washington* (SSBN-598) shortly after she successfully fired two test missiles. Rickover was excluded from the early Polaris development on orders from the Chief of Naval Operations. (U.S. Navy)

This is an artist's conception of a nuclear-propelled submarine armed with Jupiter-type ballistic missiles. Note that only four missiles are carried; these are surface-launched as the sail of the submarine breaks the water. The jagged lines indicate the use of satellite navigation by the submarine. (U.S. Navy)

The lead Polaris submarine, the *George Washington*, is launched at the Electric Boat yard on June 10, 1959. She has a lengthened *Albacore/Skipjack* hull, with a "turtle back" added to allow for the additional depth needed for the missile tubes. The hurried nature of her construction and launching, plus the intensive training requirements for the submarine's crew, led to the shortage of sailors aboard during the launching. (General Dynamics/Electric Boat)

Blue and Gold crews line up aboard the second Polaris submarine, the *Patrick Henry* (SSBN-599), during a turnover while the submarine is alongside the tender *Proteus* (AS-19) at Holy Loch, Scotland. The Polaris patrols were sixty days at sea—submerged; the submarine would then come into port and after a brief handing over of responsibilities, the alternate crew would take over for the next patrol. The incoming crew would then have leave and training in the States for almost two months. (U.S. Navy)

United States had detonated the first H-bomb. It demonstrated the Soviet Union's determination to develop strategic weapons. A White House-sponsored study recommended that as part of the American response the Army and Navy collaborate in the development of a 1,500-mile ballistic missile. The Navy was concerned with the problems of handling a large missile with hazardous liquid fuels aboard surface ships. Submarine-launched missiles seemed even further off.

The Navy established a Special Projects Office to direct development of the shipboard version of the missile, plus the related fire control, navigation, and other shipboard systems. The office was under the aegis of the most senior civilians and officers of the Navy department. Some Navy leaders opposed the missile effort, fearing that the cost would cause reductions in other, more traditional Navy programs, and there was concern that there could be another interservice controversy over roles and and missions of the Navy. The so-called carrier-versus-bomber controversy of the late 1940s had left a scar on many Navy officials as the Navy lost its plan to build a new class of large aircraft carriers. (The Korean War, however, led to a resumption of carrier construction.)

Admiral Arleigh Burke, who became Chief of Naval Operations in mid-1955, strongly supported the sea-based missile and appointed Rear Admiral William F. Raborn, Jr., to head the program. Burke gave Raborn the top people available, stopped opposition to the effort within the Navy, and made certain that Raborn had direct access to the top Navy civilians, as well as to Burke himself. The schedule for getting the missile to sea was ten years—target date: 1965.

The program began as a joint Army-Navy effort. However, in mid-1956 the Special Projects Office began work on developing a small, solid-propellant rocket engine. At the same time, the Atomic Energy Commission was producing smaller nuclear warheads. Solid propellants were less powerful than liquid rocket fuels and the smaller warhead could mean that less rocket power was needed, hence a smaller missile could be de-

The *George Washington*, still on trials, almost dead in the water on April 28, 1960. Note her "turtle back" in this view, with flush-fitting hatches for the sixteen missile tubes. While she is on deterrent patrols, the identifying hull number of her sail and the name painted amidships are blacked out as a precaution, in case the submarine makes an unplanned surfacing and is sighted by a foreign ship. (General Dynamics/Electric Boat)

The *Simon Bolivar* (SSBN-641) at high speed off Norfolk. From 1967 until 1980 the U.S. Navy had 41 of these strategic missile submarines. Subsequently, the ten older Polaris-armed submarines have been retired to had their missiles removed, reducing the SSBN force to 31 "boats" pending the first Trident submarine becoming operational in 1982. (Giorgio Arra)

The *Thomas A. Edison* (in rear) passes the *Francis Scott Key* (SSBN-657) as the two missile submarines transited the Panama Canal in 1973. The later submarine is slightly larger and has carried three successive generations of strategic missiles: the Polaris A-3, Poseidon C-3, and now Trident C-4. (U.S. Navy)

A Polaris A-2 missile streaks aloft after being fired from the submarine *Thomas A. Edison* (SSBN-610). The normal launch mode for ballistic missiles is submerged, with no part of the submarine projecting through the water. Initially the missiles were ejected by compressed air, with their rockets igniting after they cleared the water. The SSBNs now have more efficient gas-ejection systems. (U.S. Navy)

veloped. And, solid propellants were more easily and more safely handled aboard ship.

Finally, on December 8, 1956, the Navy's participation in the Army's Jupiter programs ended and on New Year's Day 1957 the Navy's solid-propellant Polaris program was formally approved. Raborn accelerated the program by predicting when advanced technology would be available in the next few years. It meant taking a considerable risk, but it could reduce the Polaris development time by several years. This was true for advanced navigation equipment, as well as for the missile; the submarine commander had to know exactly where the craft was when it launched a missile, since an error of a few miles would be compounded over the 1,500-mile flight of the Polaris. The Polaris was also being planned for launching from submarines.

Polaris development progressed rapidly. Then, on October 4, 1957, the world was shocked into the space age when the Soviet Union place a 184-pound satellite into orbit. This and subsequent Soviet space spectaculars, which were far ahead of American space efforts, coupled with Soviet missile tests during 1957, caused major concern in the U.S. Government. In particular, it was feared that Soviet missile developments could lead to an intercontinental missile force able to strike American strategic bombers on their bases, before they could be launched. Efforts were undertaken to speed up bomber reaction time (including placing some continuously in the air), and U.S. missile programs were accelerated.

The Special Projects Office took another look at the Polaris schedule; at the time 1963 was the planned date for a submarine at sea with missiles. The planned range was reduced from 1,500 nautical miles to 1,200, just enough for a submarine in the Barents Sea to strike Moscow. But could submarines to carry the missiles be constructed more rapidly? Navy and Electric Boat engineers looked at the problem and the decision was made to take the *Skipjack* SSN plans and enlarge the submarine by 180 feet, mainly with a mid-section "plug" for sixteen missile

A

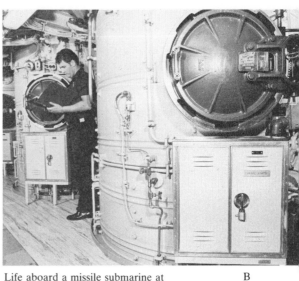

B

Life aboard a missile submarine at sea: (A) crewmen run a check on the launch operating panel; (B) Sherwood Forest—the sixteen missile tubes, with access hatches for checkout and maintenance; (C) tracing down a wiring problem in the missile control center; (D) individual bunks, each with a reading light; (E) checking out a torpedo; and (F) using one of the automatic clothes dryers. (U.S. Navy)

D

E

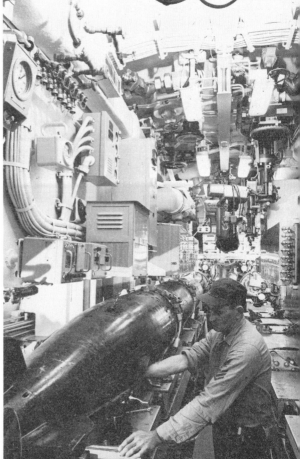

C

F

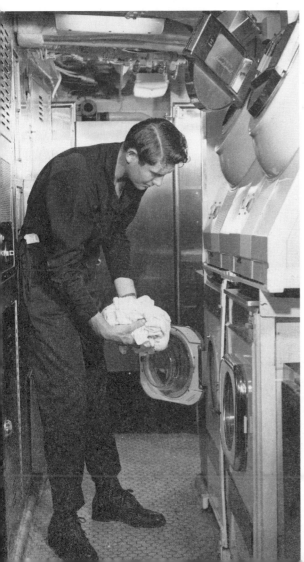

tubes. This would lengthen the submarine to just under 382 feet and increase the surface displacement to 5,900 tons. The existing S5W reactor plant could propel the submarine, albeit not as fast as a 30-knot-plus *Skipjack*.

On December 31, 1957, just a year after the Polaris project officially started, the *Scorpion* (SSN-589) under construction at Electric Boat was reordered as a ballistic missile submarine (SSBN-598), as was the not-yet-started SSN-599. The following March, construction of a third Polaris SSBN was assigned to the Mare Island Naval Shipyard. These submarines were given top priority, with three shifts of workmen being assigned for around-the-clock construction, working six and sometimes seven days a week.

In July of 1958 two more Polaris submarines were ordered from the Newport News commercial yard in Virginia, which had not constructed a submarine since the 1920s, and the Portsmouth Naval Shipyard at Kittery, Maine. Thus, four yards were involved in the Polaris program, almost from the start.

Additional Polaris submarines were soon ordered, these being 410-foot craft although retaining the basic elongated *Skipjack* hull design, S5W reactor plant, and sixteen tubes for Polaris missiles. President Eisenhower himself decided to name these submarines for distinguished Americans, with the lead ship being named the *George Washington*. The sixth submarine, introducing the second Polaris class, was the *Ethan Allen* (SSBN-608).

After several failures of test missiles, the Polaris was successfully fired, first from launch pads at Cape Canaveral and then from the missile test ship *Observation Island*. On the last day of 1959 the *George Washington* was commissioned. The following July the *George Washington* went to sea to test-fire the Polaris. Technical problems delayed the firing a day, but on July 19, 1960, the submarine successfully fired two missiles while submerged. A few minutes later the message was flashed by Admiral Raborn from the submarine at sea to President

Navy yard tugs help the *Daniel Webster* (SSBN-626) alongside a pier at the New London sub base. This is the only U.S. ballistic missile submarine with bow diving planes. (U.S. Navy, JO2 Gwyneth J. Schultz)

The *Abraham Lincoln* (SSBN-602) undergoing maintenance in the floating dry dock AFDB-7 at Holy Loch, Scotland. The Navy also had Polaris support bases at Rota, Spain, and Guam in the Marianas during the 1960s and 1970s. (U.S. Navy, PH1 Van den Handel)

Eisenhower: POLARIS—FROM OUT OF THE DEEP TO TARGET. PERFECT.

That same afternoon the Eisenhower Administration released funds previously voted by Congress to build two more Polaris submarines. This brought to fourteen the number of SSBNs fully funded. The eleventh submarine started the third Polaris class. Named *Lafayette* (SSBN-616), the submarine incorporated a number of improvements, resulting in a still larger SSBN—425 feet in length and slightly heavier.

After additional trials and missile tests, on November 15, 1960, the *George Washington* went to sea on the first American strategic deterrent patrol. Although the Soviets had already put both nuclear and diesel submarines to sea with ballistic missiles, the *George Washington* was a far superior craft, with sixteen missiles, each carrying a one-megaton warhead, that could be delivered against targets some 1,200 nautical miles away. The Soviet submarines mostly had only three missiles each, with a range of a few hundred miles, and apparently with far less accuracy than the Polaris.

An innovative manning scheme, assigning two crews to each U.S. submarine, would permit the undersea craft to spend more than half of their time at sea. While one crew was aboard, the other crew—numbering some 16 officers and 120 enlisted men—would be ashore, on leave or in training. After an SSBN completed a deployment, the other alternate crew would come aboard, there would be a brief changeover period, the submarine would be provisioned, and would go to sea while the original crew went home. Thus, some twenty-five of the forty-plus submarines would be at sea at any given time. This crew concept was called Blue-and-Gold, for the Navy's colors.

Once at sea the Polaris SSBN would cruise slowly in a patrol area, carefully avoiding contact with other submarines or surface ships. The submarine would remain on patrol for some sixty consecutive days, without transmitting radio messages that could reveal its location. However, by coming near to the surface and trailing an aerial wire through the water, the submarine could pick up messages being sent on a regular basis from the United States. These would be mainly administrative messages and "familygrams," personal word of how each man's family was doing during the cruise. The low-frequency transmissions could also carry attack orders if necessary, the encoded message initiated by the President that would order the submarines to fire. For that message two or more officers would have to "authenticate" that it was a legitimate message, and the captain and executive officer would both have to insert keys to launch the missiles. (Of course, many other crewmen would be involved in the launch procedures.)

The second Polaris submarine, the *Patrick Henry*, went to sea on patrol on December 30, 1960, bringing to thirty-two the number of combat-ready missiles at sea. At the time the total U.S. intercontinental missile (ICBM) strength was sixteen Atlas-D missiles. Fears of Soviet missile development led to a major issue of the 1960 presidential campaign being the "missile gap." Whether real or imagined, the issue emphasized the high survivability of missile submarines, especially in comparison with manned bombers.

When President Kennedy took office on January 20, 1961, he directed an immediate speedup of the Polaris program. Borrowing money from other projects, he ordered the construction of five more Polaris submarines. He then asked Congress to provide funds for another ten submarines, for a Polaris program of twenty-nine "boats." Kennedy also accelerated development of improved Polaris missiles. The A-2 model, which went to sea in late 1962, had a range of 1,500 nautical miles, and the A-3—ready for the fleet in 1964—could travel 2,500 miles. These increased ranges gave the submarines more maneuvering room while still able to strike key Soviet targets. This, in turn, would complicate Soviet anti-submarine efforts,

The A-3 also had an advanced MRV or Multiple Re-entry Vehicle warhead. As the warhead would streak toward its target it would separate into three small re-entry

The *Woodrow Wilson* (SSBN-624) tests her main ballast blow system during an alongside test at the Mare Island Naval Shipyard. Ballast tanks are filled while the submarine is on the surface to bring it to neutral buoyancy; then the craft is "driven" under with the use of diving planes. Similarly, diving planes normally are used to surface, with the ballast blow system being used in emergencies. (U.S. Navy, Myron Abrams)

This unusual view of the *Lafayette* (SSBN-616) shows the giant submarine sliding down the building ways at the Electric Boat yard moments after being christened by Mrs John F. Kennedy. Although the nuclear *Triton* was longer, the *Lafayette* was the heaviest submarine ye built. (General Dynamics/Electric Boat)

A Polaris missile is removed for checkout or repair from the *Thomas A. Edison* (SSBN-610) by the submarine tender *Hunley* (AS-31). Named for the Confederate submarine proponent, the *Hunley* is one of four new-construction tenders and one converted ship (the *Proteus*) fitted to support ballistic missile submarines. (U.S. Navy)

vehicles or "bomblets," each of about 200 kilotons. The RVs would be "shotgunned" down on a target, insuring a higher probability of destruction than if a single, large warhead struck near the target.

The Polaris submarines were able to take these improved missiles with only slight modification. Meanwhile, the Kennedy Administration and Congress approved an ultimate U.S. Polaris force of forty-one submarines carrying 656 missiles. For a brief period forty-five submarines were planned (five squadrons with nine submarines each), but budgetary problems and the availability of large numbers of land-based ICBMs led to the program being halted with forty-one submarines, the last being completed early in 1967.

Shortly before his death in November 1963, President Kennedy witnessed a Polaris test firing at sea. From the early 1960s on, the Polaris submarine force provided one leg of the so-called TRIAD, the term developed about 1970 to justify the continued deployment of three strategic systems, land-based bombers, land-based ICBMs, and missile submarines. But the submarines provided the most survivable portion of the TRIAD. And, from 1970 on, the thirty-one submarines of the *Lafayette* class were rearmed with the Poseidon C-3 missile.

The Poseidon is a MIRV—Multiple Independently-targeted Re-entry Vehicle—missile. Whereas the Polaris A-3 missile could shotgun three small nuclear weapons down on a single target to ensure more thorough destruction, the Poseidon has a "bus" or post-boost vehicle that carries several weapons to be independently targeted against separate points within the "footprint" of the bus's dispersal pattern. The bus-dispenser has navigation and maneuvering devices to shift its attitude slightly as each weapon is released, thus aligning it for the next target. The Poseidon bus is configured to carry up to fourteen small weapons of about 50 kilotons each (compared to weapons of less than 20 kilotons used at Hiroshima and Nagasaki, and one-megaton warheads in the early Polaris missiles). While

the relatively smaller Poseidon warheads have less effectiveness against hardened targets, such as underground command centers and missile silos, the large number of weapons available offers other strike advantages. The Poseidon bus is designed to carry up to fourteen weapons; however, this full loading results in a major reduction in missile range, to perhaps 2,000 nautical miles. Thus, in actual submarine deployment the Navy has armed the Poseidon missiles with only eight or ten weapons, giving slightly more range while still providing each sixteen-tube submarine with a large number of warheads. By the late 1970s, when the thirty-one *Lafayette*-class submarines were rearmed with Poseidon missiles, the Navy's submarine force contributed about 30 percent of the nation's strategic launchers. However, those 656 missiles—160 Polaris A-3 and 496 Poseidon— contributed about 70 percent of the ICBM and submarine-launched weapons that could be independently targeted against an enemy.* This consideration, coupled with the Polaris–Poseidon submarines' relatively high survivability against Soviet anti-submarine forces, made them the primary U.S. strategic-deterrent force through the 1970s and into the 1980s.

In a further effort to improve this force, from 1979 on, twelve of the *Lafayette* Poseidon-armed submarines have been further refitted to launch the Trident C-4 missiles. The Trident, with a range of some 4,000 nautical miles, carries an eight-MIRV warhead, which can deliver its weapons with much greater accuracy than previous submarine missiles. The Trident has been publicly cited as being able to deliver its eight 100-kilotons weapons with such accuracy that half the re-entry vehicles can hit a target within a 300-foot radius.

The decision to arm the last twelve *Lafayette*-class submarines with still another generation of missiles came about because of

*Three-MIRV warheads were also fitted during the 1970s to 550 of the nation's 1,000 Minuteman ICBMs. There were also 54 Titan II intercontinental missiles, each with one warhead, as were the 450 early Minuteman missiles.

A strategic missile submarine comes home after a deterrent patrol. The *Sam Rayburn* (SSBN-635) prepares to moor alongside a submarine tender at Holy Loch, Scotland. After a turn-over period of a few days, these men will be flown to their home port in the United States and the alternate crew will take the submarine to sea. (U.S. Navy)

The *Henry Clay* (SSBN-625) makes a rare surface launch of a Polaris missile. The submarine has a slight list to port as a precaution against the missile not igniting and falling back on the submarine. The tall mast is a telemetry antenna installed only during test launches off Cape Kennedy, where this firing occurred on April 20, 1964. (U.S. Navy)

Six days before his tragic death, President John F. Kennedy observed a Polaris missile launch by the *Andrew Jackson* (SSBN-619). He wrote to the Polaris project director: "The Polaris firing I witnessed. . . was a most satisfying and fascinating experience. It is still incredible to me that a missile can be successfully and accurately fired from beneath the sea. Once one has seen a Polaris firing the efficacy of this weapons system as a deterrent is not debatable." (U.S. Navy)

the long delays in completing the first of the submarines being built specifically to carry the Trident missile (see Chapter 10). The flexibility and durability of the nuclear-propelled missile submarine was thus proven, as some *Lafayette*s went through three generations of missiles—the Polaris, Poseidon, and Trident.

But at the same time, by the late 1970s the oldest of the Polaris submarines were completing their second decade of intensive operations on deterrent patrol. Based on 1950s technology, the submarines of the *George Washington* and *Ethan Allen* classes were becoming increasingly expensive to operate and maintain, while their machinery was noisier and their operating depth less than later SSBNs, increasing their potential vulnerability to enemy attack. During 1980-81 these ten oldest Polaris submarines were retired, resulting in a reduction of the Navy's submarine missile force below the 41-boat level for the first time since 1967. Although partially offset by the increase in weapons carried by the MIRV-warhead missiles, the decrease in the total number of missile tubes and submarines at sea helped contribute to the increasing concern over Soviet military advances from the late 1970s onward. It was hoped that the advanced attack and strategic missile submarines that the United States could build would compensate in quality for the shortfall in numbers, in comparison with the Soviet undersea force.

In this bow-on view, the *Thresher* presents an almost sinister appearance. Less than two years after she was commissioned, on April 10, 1963, the *Thresher* was making a post-overhaul test dive off the New England coast when she was lost with all 129 officers, civilians, and enlisted men on board. Subsequently, two more nuclear submarines have been lost—the USS *Scorpion* (SSN-589) in May 1968 with all 99 men on board, and a Soviet November-class SSN off Spain in May 1970, apparently without any casualties. (U.S. Navy)

10. THE MODERN NUCS

"The nuclear-powered submarine is not just an improved submarine, but a totally different kind of warship," Admiral Rickover once told a Congressional subcommittee. He was correct. Especially when the high-speed *Albacore* hull design was combined with the S5W nuclear propulsion plant in the *Skipjack* class, the result was a torpedo-attack submarine with virtually unlimited high-speed underwater endurance, a submarine that was a significantly more capable weapon than any previous submarine.

Still, the *Skipjack* is relatively noisy and her operating depth is comparable to World War II-built submarines. A quieter submarine, at slow speeds, is less vulnerable to acoustic (sonar) detection, while a deeper-diving submarine can take advantage of ocean temperature differences to escape detection, has more "maneuvering room" to take advantage of high speed, and with its stronger hull would be less vulnerable to enemy weapons at lesser depths. But the costs of going quieter and deeper are high.

Quieting a nuclear plant and the associated machinery requires special equipment and sound-isolation mounting of machinery, both requiring more space; a deeper diving capability means stronger hull steel and improved designs for the many pipes and wires that penetrate the submarine's pressure hull. Admiral Rickover strongly opposed the move to quieter, deeper-diving submarines, fearing their cost and complexity. But such advances were necessary in view of the improving Soviet military capabilities.

On January 15, 1958, the Navy ordered the attack submarine *Thresher* (SSN-593) from the Portsmouth Naval Shipyard. She would be the first of a new generation of quieter, deeper-diving, and otherwise more advanced nuclear submarines. To enable the *Thresher* to withstand the intense pressure of greater depths, the Navy used HY-80 steel for the first time in a submarine pressure hull. The designation HY-80 (High Yield) indicated an ability to withstand pressure of 80,000 pounds per square inch. This would

The USS *Thresher* was designed to operate deeper and more quietly than the previous U.S. nuclear submarines. The use of improved HY-80 steel, extensive sound-isolation mountings for her machinery, and other features made these characteristics possible. Like the one-of-a-kind *Tullibee*, the *Thresher* had her sonar in the bow, with four torpedo tubes angled out amidships. (U.S. Navy).

The bow sonar dome awaits installation in the *Thresher*. After installation the 15-foot-diameter sphere will be fitted with hydrophones that can be activated in sequence to provide a 360-degree search and target-tracking capability. The total *Thresher* sonar system was known as the AN/BQQ-2, and included primarily the AN/BQS-6 active sonar and AN/BQR-7 passive set. While the sub is at sea, this sphere is flooded to enhance hydroacoustic efficiency. (U.S. Navy, K.H. Grant)

A UUM-44 SUBROC (Submarine Rocket) is loaded aboard the *Permit* (SSN-594). The weapon is being loaded through the torpedo loading hatch aft of the small sail structure, to be lowered down to the amidships torpedo room. The 21-foot, 4,000-pound weapon was one of two U.S. Navy submarine-launched ASW weapons with a nuclear warhead. The other, the Mark 45 ASTOR (Anti-Submarine Torpedo), has been discarded. (U.S. Navy)

permit a *Thresher*-class submarine to operate deeper than any previous American combat submarine. The *Thresher* would have a modified *Albacore*-style hull and *Skipjack* S5W power plant, although because she was larger than the *Skipjack* she would be slower.

Inside, the *Thresher* would have a radically different arrangement than previous submarines, except for the one-of-a-kind *Tullibee*. The *Thresher* would have a sonar system or "suit" in the bow, the traditional location of a submarine's torpedo tubes. Although the earlier killer submarines had larger bow sonar installations, these were still "added" to the design, with bow torpedo tubes and other constraints affecting the sonar's design. The *Thresher* would have a large AN/BQQ-2 sonar system, consisting of a large, 15-foot-diameter sphere in the bow, mounting passive acoustic transducers of the AN/BQS-6 sonar. Complementing this passive sonar was the AN/BQR-7 active sonar that could send out an acoustic pulse for accurate measurement to distant underwater objects, such as an enemy submarine. Thus, the passive BQS-6 could detect another submarine's machinery and movement noises, with the active BQR-7 being used for the precise information needed to fire weapons. These bow-mounted portions of the BQQ-2 would be supplemented by a towed sonar array that could be streamed out behind the submarine.

With her bow taken up by the major components of the BQQ-2 sonar system, the *Thresher*'s four torpedo tubes were fitted amidships in the hull, angled out, two to each side, at an angle of about ten degrees from the centerline. These tubes could fire anti-submarine or anti-shipping torpedos, or the SUBROC—Submarine Rocket—that became operational in 1965. The SUBROC is 21 feet long and 21 inches in diameter, the same size as a modern torpedo. And, like a torpedo, it is fired from a submarine's torpedo tubes. But there the similarity ends. After being launched from the tube by compressed air a rocket motor starts in the SUBROC, propelling the missile up to the surface, and then through the air on a ballistic trajectory

The Modern Nucs / 139

The complexity of the nuclear submarine is shown in this view of the control room of the *Whale* (SSN-638). The sailors in the foreground control the *Whale*'s course and depth with aircraft-type controls. Speed, course, and depth can be automatically fed to a computer for "hands off" control while underway. (U.S. Navy)

Cutaway of *Sturgeon*-class submarine.

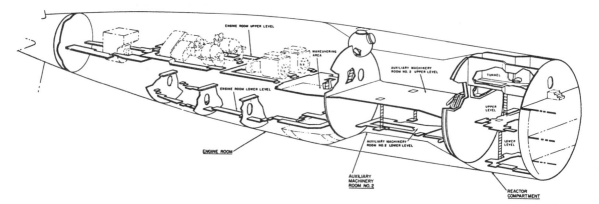

The *Barb* (SSN-596) enters Hong
Kong harbor with her Electronic
Countermeasures (ECM) mast and
periscopes extended. Modern nuclear submarines look small and
awkward on the surface; underwater
they are sleek and potent. The small
deck area requires that men on deck
wear safety lines attached to the
hull. (Giorgio Arra)

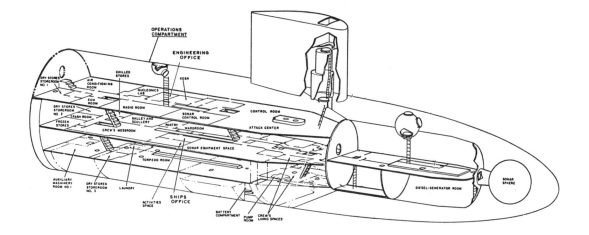

TABLE 10. LATER NUCLEAR SUBMARINES

Hull Numbers	Number Built[1]	Class	Launched	Displacement	Length Overall	Speed	Torpedo[2] Tubes	Crew
SSN–593 to 596 SSN–603 to 607 SSN–612 SSN–621	11	*Thresher* (later *Permit* class)	1960–1966	3,750/4,310	278–	~20/~30	4 21-in.	85
SSN–613 to 615	3	Modified *Permit*	1963–1964	3,800/4,600	292–	~20/~30	4 21-in.	85
SSN–597	1	*Tullibee*	1960	2,317/2,640	273	15/15+	4 21-in.	52
SSN–637 to 639 SSN–646 to 653 SSN–660 to 670 SSN–672 to 684 SSN–686 to 687	37	*Sturgeon*	1966–1974	3,640/4,650	292	~20/~30	4 21-in.	120
SSN–671	1	*Narwhal*	1966	4,450/5,350	314	~25/~30	4 21-in.	120
SSN–686	1	*Glenard P. Lipscomb*	1973	5,800/6,840	365	18/~25	4 21-in.	120
SSN–688 to 724	10+27	*Los Angeles*	1974–	6,000/6,900	360	/30+	4 21-in.	127
SSBN–726 to 734	0+8	*Ohio*	1979–	16,600/18,700	560	/20+	4 21-in.	153[3]

1. Data for *Los Angeles* and *Ohio* classes indicate number of submarines completed as of early 1981 plus number under construction (authorized through fiscal year 1981).
2. All amidships torpedo tubes.
3. Two crews assigned.

The Mark 48 is considered to be the U.S. Navy's "ultimate" torpedo. With both wire guidance from the launching submarine and self-contained sonar guidance, the Mark 48 has a range of over twenty miles. The weapon is 19 feet long, 21 inches in diameter, and weighs 3,450 pounds. By 1980 all U.S. attack and missile submarines except the *Grayback* carried the Mark 48. This is an early Mark 48 being loaded aboard an SSN at Cape Kennedy (Cape Canaveral) for a test launch. (U.S. Air Force)

A SUBROC streaks from the water after being fired from a submarine's torpedo tube. In flight the booster rocket is discarded, and then a parachute lowers a nuclear depth charge into the water some thirty miles from the launching submarine, to destroy a hostile undersea craft. (Goodyear)

to a predetermined point some 30 miles away. There the warhead—a small nuclear weapon—enters the water to destroy any enemy submarine within its lethal kill range.

The *Thresher* would be only slightly larger in displacement than the early nuclear boats, having a surface displacement of 3,750 tons. However, the modified *Albacore* hull would result in a large diameter (31⅔ feet) with a submarine length of 278½ feet. Although initially assigned a crew of 80-plus officers and men, in time the *Thresher*-class manning requirements grew to more than 120, the increases caused by the complexity of the sonar and other electronics, and the nuclear plant. Almost half of the crew of a modern SSN are assigned to the engineering plant.

The lead ship, the *Thresher*, was commissioned on August 3, 1961. Three months earlier the *Thresher* had gone to sea on her initial trials, during which she went deeper than any U.S. submarine had gone before. The trials were halted, however, before the submarine reached the rated operating depth, because of instrumentation problems. She later achieved her design operating depth. After being commissioned, the *Thresher* began a series of extensive trials, with special emphasis on the submarine's self-generated noise levels and the effectiveness of the BQQ-2 sonars. In July 1962, after a year of operations, the *Thresher* entered the Portsmouth yard for an overhaul and "tuneup" that would take nine months.

The *Thresher* went back to sea early on the morning of April 9, 1963. On board were 104 crewmen, plus Navy observers, shipyard officers, and civilian technicians for a total of 129 men. Her shallow-water dives that day were successful. The next day, in water 8,400 feet deep, the *Thresher* began her deep-water tests. During the shallow trials the submarine rescue ship *Skylark* (ASR-20) had hovered nearby. Essentially a large tug, the *Skylark* did have a McCann rescue chamber, the same device that had saved thirty-three men from the *Squalus*, perched on her fantail. The water was only some 600 feet deep, and the McCann chamber could have res-

This is one of the last photos taken of the *Scorpion*, about a month before her loss in May 1968. She is shown here at Naples, Italy. When she was at sea the railings on her diving planes, bitts and cleats on deck, and her small light mast forward would be retracted or removed to make for smooth hull lines. The sail structure provides housing for masts and periscopes, has a small bridge at the top, and mounts the diving planes. There is no conning-tower compartment as in older submarines. (U.S. Navy, LT John R. Holland)

The *Glenard P. Lipscomb* returns to New London after a five-month deployment at sea. There is a harbor tug off her portside. Note the small sonar dome on the *Lipscomb*'s bow, the bitts and cleats that retract when at sea, and the bulge of a special sonar dome on the top of the sail. (U.S. Navy, Jean Russell)

The *Glenard P. Lipscomb* (SSN-685) on the surface during sea trials, turning up 17.5 knots. The *Lipscomb* engineering plant provides for nuclear–electric-drive turbines rather than the nuclear–steam turbines in all other U.S. nuclear submarines except the *Tullibee*. This makes the *Lipscomb* quieter, but slower and larger than contemporary SSNs. (General Dynamics/Electric Boat)

The *Hawkbill* (SSN-666) with several of her masts and periscopes raised. An AN/BPS-15 radar is in the raised position just beneath the American flag. An AN/BQR-26 sonar dome has been fitted to the forward edge of the sail structure. (Giorgio Arra)

An attack submarine loads Mk 48 Mod 1 torpedoes at Port Canaveral in preparation for firing trials. (U.S. Air Force)

cued survivors should the submarine have plunged to the bottom.

But in water 8,400 deep, the submarine simply could not survive a plunge to the bottom. Indeed, the McCann chamber could not even rescue men from a submarine sunk at a thousand feet, and the *Thresher's* collapse depth, that is, the maximum at which her hull and fittings were expected to survive (nominally half again the submarine's designed operating depth) was deeper.

On the morning of April 7 the *Thresher* began a test dive to her designed operating depth. Above her the *Skylark* stood by, mainly to warn shipping that there was a submarine conducting tests in the area. The only communications link between the two ships was an acoustic telephone, which produced unreliable and difficult-to-understand voice transmissions.

As the *Thresher* approached her test depth that morning she reported experiencing a "minor difficulty." Lieutenant Commander John W. Harvey, her commanding officer, attempted an emergency surfacing. But the submarine could not be surfaced, and instead within a few minutes the submarine plunged out of control, into the depths beyond her collapse or crush depth, where her hull "imploded" or blew in. The debris of the submarine and the remains of 129 men rained down on the ocean floor.

The *Skylark*, not fully aware of what was happening, after a while began to suspect a problem. But her efforts to communicate with the *Thresher* were in vain, as was the massive air search subsequently undertaken by the Navy. Not until late May did ocean survey ships recover some minor items of debris. Then the deep-diving bathyscaph *Trieste* was able to photograph the partial remains of the *Thresher*.

Her loss brought a shock to the U.S. Navy and to the nation as a whole. It was the worst peacetime submarine disaster in history, and the first loss of a nuclear submarine. The exact cause of her loss will probably never be known. The official Navy inquiry indicates that a flooding casualty drove her to a depth from which she never recovered. Possibly the

A UGM-48 Harpoon anti-ship missile streaks skyward from a submerged SSN. Operational in U.S. warships since 1977, the Harpoon is a cruise or guided missile that can be fired from standard 21-inch-diameter submarine torpedo tubes against enemy ships some sixty miles away. However, with only four torpedo tubes and a limited number of reloads, modern American submarines lack flexibility in weapons capability. (McDonnell Douglas)

Serving as commander of a nuclear-powered missile submarine is a difficult and exacting assignment. Here the commanding officer of the *John C. Calhoun* (SSBN-630), Thomas A. Jewell, maneuvers his submarine alongside the tender at Holy Loch, Scotland. (U.S. Navy)

Submariners—officers and enlisted men—undergo long and arduous training programs. Here an instructor at the Naval Submarine School in New London, Connecticut, explains the workings of a nuclear reactor plant (he is pointing to one of the ship's service turbine generators that produces electricity for the submarine). Submariners also undergo reactor training at several land prototypes of submarine plants. (U.S. Navy)

jet-stream of inrushing water short-circuited critical electrical equipment. However, the submarine's "minor difficulty" that led to her going deeper and the subsequent piping failure was apparently an automatic shutdown or "scram" of the reactor plant. Then, unable to quickly restart the reactor or switch to emergency electric batteries, the submarine drifted deeper. But the *Thresher*'s loss revealed other problems with modern U.S. nuclear submarines, including inadequate stored air pressure for blowing dry ballast tanks for emergency surfacing.

These and other problems were worked on, resulting in major changes and delays in the thirteen later submarines of the class, which subsequently became known as the *Permit* (SSN-594) class, for the second submarine of the design. The *Thresher-Permit* became the basis for future American attack submarines, with the deep-diving HY-80 construction also being applied to the *Lafayette*-class ballistic missile submarines.

The thirteen *Permit*s were rapidly followed by thirty-seven submarines of the improved and slightly larger *Sturgeon* (SSN-637) class. With the same weapons and sonars, these slightly larger submarines also had the S5W power plant, meaning that there was some loss in speed. This speed factor would become a major issue during the 1970s and 1980s with the subsequent SSN classes.

During the period of the *Sturgeon* completions, 1967-75, the Navy also built two one-of-a-kind submarines, the *Narwhal* (SSN-671) and the *Glenard P. Lipscomb* (SSN-685). Both also had the basic *Thresher-Permit-Sturgeon* configuration, weapons, and sonars, but had significantly different propulsion plants. The *Narwhal*'s natural-circulation S5G reactor plant used convection to move the reactor water coolant at low speeds, thus alleviating the need for pumps, a prime source of submarine machinery noise. (At higher speeds the pumps would still be needed.) The *Narwhal* plant served as the basis for the S8G reactor plant of later missile submarines. The larger, more expensive, and slower *Lipscomb* marked another

attempt at reducing a nuclear submarine's self-generated noise, in this case substituting turbine-electric drive for the standard geared steam turbines of all previous SSNs except the *Tullibee*.

The *Lipscomb* has proved successful, being significantly quieter than other nuclear boats, but at the cost of several knots of speed over contemporary submarines, and with a much higher price tag. Admiral Rickover sought to have the Navy construct three major classes of "attack" submarines during the 1970s: more of the *Lipscomb*, slow, quiet, torpedo-armed SSNs; a high-speed craft, redressing the loss of speed in SSNs since the *Skipjack* class; and a large submarine armed with anti-ship cruise missiles and powered by a 60,000-horsepower reactor plant. That plant would have four times the power of the widely used S5W plant and twice the 30,000 horsepower of the high-speed submarine. Neither the Department of Defense nor the Navy's leadership felt that the three classes could be constructed within the available budgets and force-level plans.

By 1970 the U.S. Navy had in service a total of forty-five nuclear attack submarines:

> 1 *Nautilus*
> 1 *Seawolf*
> 4 *Skate*
> 1 *Halibut* (employed in research)
> 5 *Skipjack*
> 13 *Permit*
> 1 *Narwhal*
> 1 *Lipscomb*
> 18 *Sturgeon*

The *Scorpion* (SSN-589) had been lost at sea with her entire crew of ninety-nine men in May 1968 while some 400 miles southwest of the Azores, en route back to the United States from the Mediterranean. The giant, one-time radar picket *Triton* was laid up in reserve, having been decommissioned in May 1969. In addition to the forty-five active SSNs, there were also in service the forty-one Polaris missile submarines (plus fifty-nine diesel submarines—fourteen of postwar construction, including the experimental *Alba-*

The *Los Angeles* (SSN-688) is the latest class of U.S. nuclear attack submarines. A large, 30,000-shaft horsepower reactor gives her a relatively high speed despite her large size. Her AN/BQQ-5 sonar suite is an upgraded AN/BQQ-2 of the previous U.S. SSNs. The older sets are being upgraded to the BQQ-5 capabilities during overhauls. Armament of the *Los Angeles* remains the same as previous SSN classes. Thus, the additional displacement (and relative cost) is due to the quest for a few more knots. (Newport News Shipbuilding and Dry Dock)

The *Los Angeles*-class submarine *Omaha* (SSN-692) at sea in the Pacific, with several masts and both periscopes raised. The submarine's Type 2 attack scope has a very narrow head, while the larger Type 18 is fitted for photography, and has built-in antennas for communications, satellite and other navigation, and electronic countermeasures. (Giorgio Arra)

Another *Los Angeles*-class submarine, the *Atlanta* (SSN-712), slides down the building ways at Newport News. Part of the submarine's crew, standing on a deck platform, the diving planes, and bridge, salute smartly as thousands of balloons are released. Nuclear-submarine keel layings, launchings, and commissionings have become major political events. (Newport News Shipbuilding and Dry Dock, John Frankavella)

core and *Dolphin*, and forty-five modernized war-built submarines).

The first of the high-speed submarines, the *Los Angeles* (SSN-688), was laid down on January 8, 1972, at Newport News. By that time the reduced submarine building programs, shipyard problems, and Navy–industry conflicts had reduced the nation's submarine construction yards to two, the commercial yard at Newsport News, Virginia, and the Electric Boat yard at Groton, Connecticut. The Navy's Mare Island and Portsmouth yards, and the private General Dynamics yard at Quincy, Massachusetts and the Ingalls yard in Mississippi were no longer building subs, and the New York Shipbuilding Corporation near Philadelphia had gone out of business.

As the U.S. Navy reached the force level of eighty-six nuclear attack submarines in 1970, the Soviet Navy attained a similar force level. More significant, the U.S. construction rate of nuclear submarines was declining while that of the Soviet Union was increasing (with five yards producing nuclear submarines in the 1970s and beyond).

The high-speed *Los Angeles* class, it was hoped, would provide a qualitative compensation for the Soviet leadership in numbers of submarines.* The American SSNs were primarily anti-submarine craft, intended in wartime to patrol off enemy ports and in critical water passages to intercept Soviet undersea craft. Subsequently, as the Soviets put advanced missile submarines to sea, American SSNs were given the added task of attempting to trail the enemy craft. In addition, SSNs have proven effective as clandestine reconnaissance platforms, employing various electronic/signal intelligence (ELINT/SIGINT) equipment.

Finally, because of their relatively high speed, the *Los Angeles*-class submarines are described as having another mission capability: that of aircraft carrier escort. In this role the SSN serves as a forward long-range de-

tection platform to identify and attack hostile submarines. The concept goes back many years, although it came into vogue in the 1970s mainly to help justify the construction of additional *Los Angeles*-class submarines. However, there are several problems in employing SSNs to support carrier task forces, related mainly to the limitations on communications between the carrier, her escorting ships and aircraft, and the submarine. Real-time (instantaneous) communications to and from a submarine are difficult at best, with the submarine commander rarely wanting to transmit for fear of revealing his position to an enemy. At the same time, there is continued concern that carrier aircraft or escorts will mistake the friendly SSN for an enemy. (In World War II at least two U.S. submarine were sunk by friendly forces.)

The USS *Los Angeles* was commissioned on November 13, 1976. Although she resembled the previous *Permit* and *Sturgeon* classes in appearance and internal layout, she was significantly larger—6,000 tons on the surface and 360 feet in length. The additional space and weight was taken up mainly by the S6G reactor plant, which produces a reported 30,000 horsepower, capable of returning to American SSNs the speeds lost since the *Skipjack* class, when a succession of classes grew in size while retaining the 15,000-horsepower S5W plant.

Although similar in design to the previous SSN classes, the *Los Angeles* does have the improved AN/BQQ-5 sonar suite and an advanced underwater fire control system for guiding torpedoes (with older, AN/BQQ-2 submarines subsequently being upgraded to the same equipment). New weapons also became available to complement the new sensors in the *Los Angeles* and the updated submarines. The older conventional torpedoes and the Mark 45 ASTOR (nuclear warhead) have been replaced by the Mark 48 in all U.S. submarines; this is a large, 3,450-pound, 19-foot-long torpedo with a conventional, high-explosive warhead. The Mark 48 has a range estimated at more than 20 miles, with a sophisticated guidance that can use active or passive homing, coupled with wire guidance

*In addition to some 85 nuclear submarines, at the time the Soviet Navy had approximately 250 diesel-electric submarines in service, all of postwar construction.

A Trident ballistic missile streaks aloft from the submarine *Francis Scott Key*. The antenna mast, barely visible to the left of the plume, is used only for missile range launches. (U.S. Air Force)

The Trident ballistic missile submarines are the largest undersea craft yet built in the United States. This is the *Michigan* (SSBN-727) on the assembly way at Electric Boat. The size and complexity of the Trident submarines, along with Navy management problems and shipyard difficulties, have put these submarines several years behind schedule. (General Dynamics/Electric Boat)

from the launching submarine, to seek out an enemy undersea craft or surface ship. And, the modern submarines also have SUBROC, the underwater-launched ballistic missile with a nuclear warhead.

From 1977 onward U.S. attack submarines have also been fitted to carry the Harpoon anti-ship cruise missile. The Harpoon is the first American weapon designed for shipboard use against enemy warships since the Regulus I, deployed in the 1950s. The missile is designed for launching from a variety of surface ships, from aircraft, and from the torpedo tubes of conventional submarines. The submarine-launched Harpoon is loaded in an encasing capsule that is fired from the torpedo tube and rises to the surface, where the missile ignites and leaves the cannister. The missile has a range of 60 miles, with the submarine being able to fire against a target based on acoustic detection, electronic intercepts, or information from other sources (aircraft, surface ships, and in the future satellites). As the missile nears the target it uses active radar to seek out the target.

Harpoon provides U.S. submarines with a long-range capability against surface ships, complementing the Mark 48 torpedo for this purpose. The Harpoon, however, can only be carried and fired in limited numbers because of the small number of torpedo tubes (four) in *Permit* and later SSNs, and the perhaps two dozen reload spaces available for torpedoes, SUBROCs, and decoys/noisemakers as well as Harpoons.

Also under development in the late 1970s was the Tomahawk cruise missile, a larger weapon than the Harpoon, but still capable of being fired from a submarine torpedo tube. The Tomahawk Anti-Ship Missile (T-ASM) would have a range of several hundred miles with a 1,000-pound high-explosive warhead, or perhaps, 2,000 miles or more with a small nuclear warhead in the Land-Attack Missile (T-LAM). The long-range capabilities of the Tomahawk place still more demands on the submarine, which must locate and identify targets.

The need to carry more weapons in attack submarines led to a Navy decision in 1981 to arm the *Los Angeles*-class boats with twelve Tomahawk tubes external to the pressure hull, in space previously used for some of the bow ballast tanks. This would in effect make them combined torpedo-attack/cruise-missile submarines.

Another weapon under development since the late 1970s for possible submarine application has been the SIAM (Self-Initiating Anti-aircraft Missile). This weapon is the latest attempt to produce a suitable weapon for a submarine to attack ASW helicopters of fixed-wing aircraft. The SIAM would be fired from special tubes in the submarine after the aircraft is initially detected by acoustic means. After launching, the missile searches for and acquires the target aircraft. (The Royal Navy previously developed an anti-aircraft missile fired from a launcher that extends from the submarine's sail above the water; dubbed SLAM for Submarine-Launched Air Missile, it is used in Israeli submarines.)

Development of the Harpoon and Tomahawk has led to increased interest in developing a submarine with more than the four weapon tubes of recent American SSNs. At the same time, the high costs of the *Los Angeles* class have caused the Navy to seek alternative SSN designs, possibly giving up the large S6G reactor and a few knots of speed gained over the previous attack submarine classes. Although speed is significant, the high dollar cost and the possibility that improved sensors and weapons could compensate for the few knots' advantage have become pressing issues. Also while 30-plus-knot SSNs are "better" in some respects than slower submarines, they still cannot close with the high-speed Soviet submarines of the Alfa class, rated in the press at forty-three knots, and possibly other high-speed Soviet undersea craft. Indeed, advanced technology and construction techniques could lead to a new-design SSN, smaller than a *Los Angeles*, with the same speed, weapons, and sensors.

There are several parallels between some of the current attack-submarine issues and those related to the Trident strategic missile

The modern submarine: The USS
Los Angeles (SSN-688) – the latest
and best submarine that the U.S.
Navy has been able to produce.
(Giorgio Arra)

The attack submarine *Birmingham*
(SSN-695) breaks through the surface during a test of the submarine's
emergency surfacing capabilities.
(U.S. Navy)

submarine. The Trident is the only U.S. strategic weapon that was approved for deployment during the 1970s. The Trident was conceived in 1966-67 by the STRAT-X study sponsored by the Department of Defense to determine preferred U.S. strategic systems for the 1980s and beyond. The STRAT-X study proposed an SSBN of some 8,250 tons, about 445 feet long, with missiles carried horizontally, external to the pressure hull. This arrangement would have permitted a submarine smaller than a similar craft with vertical tubes, and would allow more rapid updating of missiles. Such a submarine did not require a large power plant because SSBNs were to steam slowly in mid-ocean. The STRAT-X submarine would be carrying a missile with a range of 6,000 nautical miles.

Following the STRAT-X study, the Department of Defense and Navy developed a plan to initially build ten submarines to become operational from 1978 to 1981, as the oldest Polaris submarines began retiring. The Trident program, however, has slowed far behind the original schedule, both in missile development and submarine construction. The planned 6,000-nautical-mile missile would have been able to strike the Soviet Union from vast submarine operating areas, greatly complicating Soviet ASW. Instead, the Navy opted for a missile range of only 4,000 miles, in part because of limits on funds and technical resources, a desire to use the same firm that had developed the Polaris and Poseidon missiles, and to have the Trident missile fit into existing Poseidon submarines, in part to overcome the delays being encountered with the new Trident SSBNs. The Trident program was split into the C-4 missile, with a range of 4,000 miles, and the D-5, to have a range of 6,000 miles with the same eight-MIRV warhead. Only the first version has been developed, going to sea for the first time in the fall of 1979 aboard the USS *Francis Scott Key* (SSBN-657). The later Trident missile became a long-term development project.

The Trident submarine itself was to be the largest undersea craft ever attempted, although major delays enabled the Soviet Navy to complete the first of the larger Typhoon-class SSBNS first. The Trident SSBN was designed with a surface displacement of 16,600 tons, or roughly twice that of the earlier *Lafayette*-class submarines. But while the former carried sixteen Poseidon missiles, the Trident SSBN would have a twenty-four-missile battery, initially the C-4 missile and—when developed—the longer-range D-5. The Trident's size was also due, in part, to the S8G reactor plant, the largest yet provided to an American submarine, with unofficial horsepower estimates as high as 60,000 horsepower, or twice that of the *Los Angeles* SSN. The rationale for this horsepower is difficult to divine, for should the SSBN speed up to escape a pursuing submarine or surface ship, the craft's noise level increases, thus increasing the ranges at which an enemy could detect the submarine.*

The lead Trident submarine, to be named *Ohio* (SSBN-726), was ordered from the Electric Boat yard in 1974. At that time the planned delivery for the first submarine was April 1979, but a clause was inserted in the schedule noting that "In recognition of the high national priority assigned to the Trident program the contractor has promised to use his best efforts to support a Dec[ember] 1977 delivery date for the lead ship."

Soon delays began being announced in the construction of the *Ohio* and subsequent Trident SSBNs ordered from Electric Boat. The delays continued despite Electric Boat working three shifts a day on weekdays and one shift on Saturdays. But there have been continual problems in the shipyard, in the contractor-supplied materials, and in the Navy's management of the Trident program. The last led to charges and countercharges by Admiral Rickover and the Secretary of the Navy, threats by the shipyard to stop all work on the Trident submarines, and confusion over just which Navy office was "in charge" of the program

The 1979 completion date passed, with the

*Although when planned the Trident was to be the world's largest submarine with a submerged displacement of 18,700 tons, in 1980 the USSR launched the first Typhoon-class SSBN, which was estimated to displace about 25,000 tons submerged.

The one-of-a-kind *Narwhal* (SSN-671) has a natural-circulation S5G reactor plant. The submarine is quieter at slower speeds than submarines with the S5W plant. Features of her plant were incorporated in the later *Los Angeles* and Trident submarine classes. (General Dynamics/Electric Boat)

The USS *L. Mendel Rivers* (SSN-686) at sea. Submarines like the *Rivers* have an important role in American political and military strategy, and shall continue to for the foreseeable future. (Newport News Shipbuilding and Dry Dock)

560-foot *Ohio* being launched on April 7 of that year. Subsequent schedule revisions have placed the completion of the *Ohio* in 1981-82. By that time the retirement of the first ten Polaris submarines will have reduced the American SSBN force to thirty-one submarines, admittedly with improved missiles (see Chapter 9).

Through fiscal year 1981, a total of nine *Ohio*-class SSBNs had been ordered from Electric Boat, with the last having a planned 1986 completion date. There is a requirement for additional sea-based strategic missiles for deployment in the 1990s and beyond, especially with the delays encountered in procuring the advanced land-based strategic missile (MX) and an advanced land-based strategic bomber.

As in the SSN program, by the start of the 1980s some Defense and Navy officials were looking toward a smaller and less costly Trident missile submarine. One proposal put forth calls for converting some of the not-yet-started *Los Angeles*-class SSNs to a Trident-armed configuration, much the same as the *Skipjack* design was modified into the original Polaris class. Other proposals include a smaller Trident SSBN with a *Narwhal* (S5G) or *Los Angeles* (S6G) reactor plant, possibly carrying only twenty or even sixteen missiles.

In both the attack submarine and strategic missile programs there will be a continuing need for development and construction, for submarines, especially nuclear submarines, will continue to have a vital role in American defense policy for the foreseeable future.

The ten oldest Polaris submarines were removed from the nation's strategic attack force in the early 1980s with two being immediately mothballed and the eight others employed as interim torpedo-attack submarines. This is the *Patrick Henry* as SSN-599, leaving Charleston, S.C., in 1982. These former SSBNs began to decommission in 1983. (Giorgio Arra)

Admiral H.G. Rickover, flanked by Senator John Glenn of Ohio and the Atlantic Fleet commander, Admiral Harry Train, board the USS *Ohio* for her commissioning on November 11, 1981. Two days later Rickover was asked to step down by Secretary of the Navy John Lehman, ending his almost three decades of directing the Navy's nuclear propulsion program. (N. Polmar)

Increased capabilities of the *Ohio* make her a more complex submarine than previous undersea craft. This is the control room of the submarine. (U.S. Navy, PH1 Dale Anderson)

The size of the Trident SSBN is shown dramatically in this view of the *Ohio* (SSBN-726) shown fitting out alongside the attack submarine *Jacksonville* (SSN-699). The *Jacksonville* is only twenty feet shorter than the first American SSBNs, but 200 feet shorter than the giant Trident SSBNs. The *Ohio*'s twenty-four missile tubes are open and a shed covers the submarine's bow during sonar installation. (General Dynamics/Electric Boat)

The giant *Ohio* at sea for the first time on trials in June 1981. At the time Admiral Rickover charged that this photograph, released by the General Dynamics Corporation without his personal approval, "represents both a serious breach of security and willful violation of terms of the contract [to build the submarine]. Similar photographs were taken by scores of persons as the giant submarine moved down the Thames River toward Long Island Sound. (General Dynamics)

Heading to sea: The USS *Flasher* (SSN-613) departs the naval base at Charleston, S.C., heading down channel for the open sea. (Giorgio Arra)

The *Alvin* in flight. The *Alvin* was the first of three similar deep submergence vehicles that, despite their "cute" appearance, have been most useful in naval and scientific missions. Viewing ports are visible at the bow and the propulsion-maneuvering propellers atop the craft and at the stern. (Woods Hole Oceanographic Research Institution)

Appendix A
DEEP SUBMERGENCE VEHICLES

U.S. Navy operations with deep submergence vehicles began early in 1957 when the Office of Naval Research chartered the bathyscaph *Trieste* for a series of scientific dives in the Mediterranean. The term *bathyscaph* (Greek for *deep boat*) indicates a submersible with great vertical range, but little horizontal mobility; what one American has called an "ocean elevator."

The original *Trieste* was built by Professor Auguste Piccard, a Swiss scientist known for his high-altitude balloon flights as well as underwater endeavors. The bathyscaph *Trieste* was completed in the Italian seaport of that name in 1953. The two-man craft had a forged steel pressure sphere, attached to the bottom of a float that could hold approximately 25,000 gallons of gasoline. The gasoline, being lighter than water, would serve to lift the craft to the surface after ballast was jettisoned. Ballast was provided by nine tons of iron shot, carried in two tubs within the float, and restrained by electromagnets. Thus, if power failed the magnets would lose their restraining ability. Two electric motors could propel the *Trieste* at about one knot for four hours on a horizontal plane. With its original Terni sphere the *Trieste* was credited with a 20,000-foot depth, sufficient to enable her to explore some 98 percent of the ocean floor.

The 1957 dives of the *Trieste* sponsored by the U.S. Navy led to outright purchase of the craft in 1958. Significantly, two Navy lieutenants, both submariners, were placed in charge of the craft, attesting to the Navy's intention to use the *Trieste* to support fleet operations. Shortly after being purchased, the *Trieste*'s pressure sphere was replaced by another fabricated at the Krupp plant in Essen, Germany. This sphere, with an internal diameter of six feet and a wall thickness of five inches, was intended to reach a depth of 36,000 feet, the deepest known in the earth's oceans. To support the heavier sphere, the float's capacity was increased to 34,000 gallons of gasoline.

Piloted by Lieutenant Don Walsh and

Cutaway view of the original *Trieste* configuration.

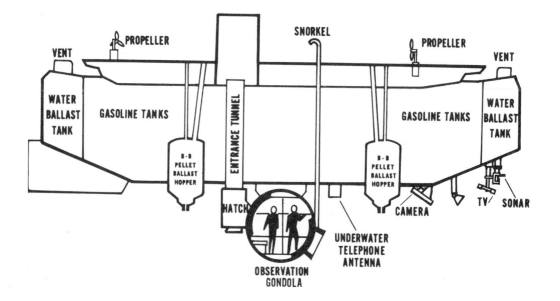

The *Trieste* in her original U.S. Navy configuration being lowered into the water. The gasoline tanks were filled to avoid breaking the "back" of the craft when lifted free of the water. Note the sphere with the access trunk leading through the float to the water shield resembling a small conning tower. The sphere or gondola has a single large viewing port opposite of the access hatch. (U.S.Navy)

This is a "fish-eye" view looking down into the sphere or gondola of the *Trieste*. The inside diameter is 6½ feet. Note the research equipment stuffed into the space along with two naval officers. Several-hour missions in the *Trieste* are uncomfortable, but provide invaluable information for naval and scientific activities. (U.S. Navy)

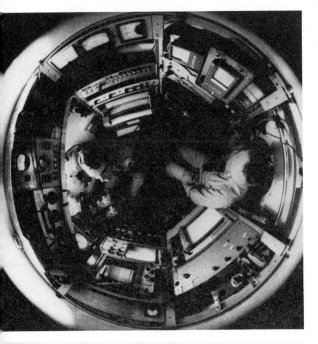

Jacques Piccard, son of Auguste, the *Trieste* descended to a depth of 35,800 feet in the Marianas Trench off Guam on January 23, 1960. This dive was part of a Navy program of studying the ocean depths for scientific, as well as military, purposes. After the Marianas dive, the *Trieste* was used for a number of Navy projects, including the recovery of objects from the ocean floor, and the searches for the sunken submarines *Thresher* and *Scorpion*.

The development of improved underwater lights and sensors, recovery devices, and other equipment led to the being rebuilt in 1963-64 at the Mare Island Naval shipyard, with a new sphere rated at 20,000 feet replacing the deeper-diving Krupp sphere. In this configuration the craft was renamed *Trieste II*. She was again rebuilt in 1965-66, and extensively modified again in 1967, all at Mare Island, as new equipment became available. Thus, the current *Trieste II* is actually a "third-generation" bathyscaph.* Based at San Diego, as part of Submarine Development Group 1, the *Trieste II* continues to support various Navy activities.

The limited horizontal mobility of the *Trieste*, and the large number of ocean research projects of interest to the Navy, led to subsequent construction of the *Alvin*, a research submersible completed for the Navy in 1965. Named for Allan Vine of the Woods Hole Oceanographic Institution in Maine, the craft is operated for the Navy by that organization. The *Alvin* has a three-man pressure sphere embedded in a streamlined hull, with an overall length of 22½ feet. The original configuration permitted operations to a depth of 6,000 feet, with a later titanium sphere doubling that capability. However, her horizontal mobility is limited, with electric motors providing a speed of about two knots for one hour, or one knot for eight hours.

When the *Alvin* was built, two additional steel spheres were constructed, one as a

*The *Trieste* is rarely referred to by her hull number. The designation X-2 was assigned in 1969 (the X-1 being a midget submarine); this was changed to DSV-1 (for Deep Submergence Vehicle) in 1971.

TABLE 11. DEEP SUBMERGENCE VEHICLES

Hull Number[1]	Name	Launched	Weight	Length	Depth	Crew[2]
—	*Trieste*	1953	150	59½	[4]	2+1
DSV–1[3]	*Trieste II*	[4]	300	78	20,000	2+1
DSV–2	*Alvin*	1964	16	22½	6,000[5]	1+2
DSV–3	*Turtle*	1968	21	26	6,500	2+1
DSV–4	*Sea Cliff*	1968	21	26	6,500[6]	2+1
DSRV–1	*Mystic*	1970	37	49⅔	5,000	3+24[7]
DSRV–2	*Avalon*	1971	37	49⅔	5,000	3+24
NR–1	—	1969	/400	136½	~3,000	5+2
HTV	—	?		153[8]	3,000+	

1. DSV hull numbers assigned in 1971 to three previously unnumbered craft.
2. Operators plus scientists.
3. Assigned hull number X–2 from 1969 until changed to DSV–1 in 1971.
4. See text.
5. Subsequently fitted with titanium sphere to provide 12,000-foot capability.
6. Being refitted with titanium sphere to provide 20,000-foot capability.
7. Carries twenty-four rescuees.
8. Tentative length.

The DSRV-1 goes to sea for a mission aboard the attack submarine *Pintado* (SSN-672). The U.S. Navy's two DSRVs are the most capable deep submergence vehicles in existence anywhere, except for the NR-1, with its longer endurance and greater payload. The white markings on the *Pintado*'s sail are to assist the DSRV during the underwater rendezvous of the two craft. (U.S. Navy, PH1 A.C. Legare)

This is the improved *Trieste II*. The float is larger and more efficient for underwater mobility, while the multiple propellers-in-rings at the stern enhance maneuvering. The "legs" project beneath the sphere to prevent it being buried when the craft sits on the ocean floor. (U.S. Navy)

When she is on the surface, relatively little of the *Trieste* is visible. Here the craft wallows on the surface, awaiting a support ship. Note the small propellers for underwater maneuvering. The kite-like affair is a radar reflector to help support ships locate the low-lying craft. (U.S. Navy)

This is the stern of the *Sea Cliff*, shown being hoisted aboard a support ship. Except for the nuclear-propelled NR-1 all deep submergence vehicles are carried to and from operating areas aboard surface ships or submarines. (General Dynamics/ Electric Boat)

spare and one for testing. The Navy later used these in two similar vehicles, the *Turtle* and *Sea Cliff*, both completed in 1969. As built, these craft have a 6,500-foot depth, with the *Sea Cliff* being refitted with a titanium sphere for 20,000-foot operations.

The Navy's next series of submersibles was much more ambitious, sparked in part by the *Thresher* disaster of April 1963. After the submarine's loss the Secretary of the Navy formed a study group to investigate Navy capabilities and requirements in the deep-ocean environment. This group recommended a major effort to develop search, rescue, small-object recovery, and submarine salvage systems. Of particular interest were means to rescue men trapped in submarines at the limits of their hull survivability. An operating depth of 5,000 feet was proposed.

The Navy's Special Projects Office, which had already made several efforts to develop deep-ocean technology to support the Polaris and Poseidon programs, was initially assigned responsibility for the new systems, collectively known as the Deep Submergence Systems Project. The Project was established in June 1964 and was made a separate Navy organization in February 1966, initially under the direction of Dr. John Craven, chief scientist of the Polaris–Poseidon programs. Two types of submersibles were called for: Deep Submergence Rescue Vehicles (DSRV) to take men off sunken submarines, and Deep Submergence Search Vehicles (DSSV) for research, search, and recovery missions down to 20,000 feet.

These would be the most advanced submersibles yet attempted by any nation. The DSRVs were designed for quick-reaction, world-wide rescue of stricken submarines. Upon notification that a submarine is disabled, a DSRV and its support equipment (the equipment being housed in a mobile van) would be loaded aboard C-141 or C-5 transport aircraft and flown to a port near the disabled submarine. At the port, the DSRV and certain equipment from the van would be placed aboard a surface ship or a

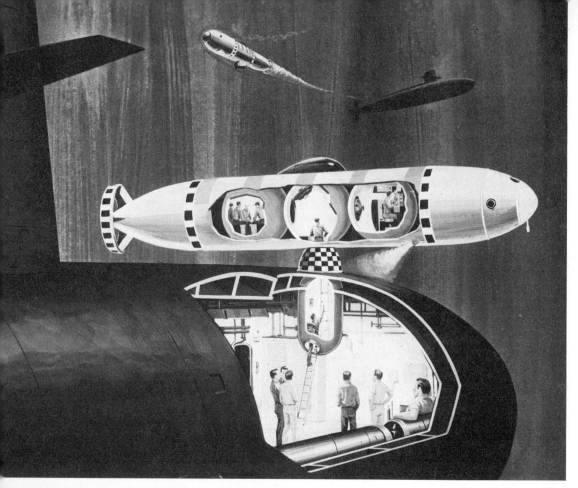

This artist's concept shows how the DSRV would operate during a rescue operation, using another submerged submarine as a floating base. Up to twenty-four survivors could be removed from the stricken craft on each shuttle trip, with emergency supplies brought aboard on the return trip. The DSRVs can operate to the maximum survival depths of U.S. submarine pressure hulls. (U.S. Navy)

This view of the DSRV *Mystic* under construction at the Lockheed facility at Sunnyvale, California, shows the three-sphere pressure capsule being installed in the fiberglass outer hull. The outer hull, which contains propulsion, sensor, and other equipment, is free flooding, making the craft much lighter than if those components were carried in a (larger) pressure hull. (Lockheed Missiles and Space)

A DSRV is unloaded from an Air Force C-5A Galaxy transport. The DSRVs are transported on special trailers that can be towed by standard truck tractors. Thus, the DSRVs are air, road, ship, and submarine transportable, to provide rapid transit to the scene of a submarine sinking. (U.S. Navy)

The NR-1 being launched at the Electric Boat yard on January 25, 1969. The craft has a submarine-like appearance, with a small sail structure and sail-mounted diving planes. However, it is a relatively short-range craft, albeit with significantly greater range than any other submersible yet constructed. (General Dynamics/Electric Boat)

"mother" submarine. The latter would be a nuclear combat submarine, modified to carry and support the DSRV.

The mother submarine, with the DSRV attached to her outer hull, would proceed to the disabled submarine and serve as an underwater base for the DSRV while the submersible transferred survivors from the disabled submarine. The mother submarine could launch and recover the DSRV while submerged and, if necessary, while under ice. The operation would be independent of surface sea or weather conditions.

The DSRV consists of three interconnected steel spheres which form the manned pressure capsule. These are housed in an outer hull of formed fiberglass. The forward 7½-foot-diameter sphere is the control compartment, manned by a pilot and copilot. The center and after spheres can accommodate twenty-four passengers and a third crewman. Under the DSRV's center sphere is a hemispherical protrusion or "skirt" that seals over the disabled submarine's hatch or the mother submarine's hatch, thus permitting passage to and from the DSRV at the same pressure as the submarine to which it is mated.

Electric motors are linked to a stern propeller and two tunnel (ducted) thrusters in the DSRV's hull, to provide a high degree of maneuverability so that the craft can mate with a disabled submarine lying at an angle. Endurance for the 37-ton, 49⅔-foot craft is eight hours, at the maximum speed of four knots.

The Navy's original plan called for twelve such vehicles, each to carry a dozen survivors per trip back to the mother submarine. But when the DSRV was enlarged to carry twenty-four passengers, the plan was cut to six craft (two to be based at each of three U.S. ports). However, rising costs, the shift of interest and resources to the Vietnam War, and reduced emphasis on oceanography and related activities led to only two DSRVs being actually built: the *Mystic*, completed in 1971, and the *Avalon*, finished a year later. At this writing the DSRVs have not yet been called upon to undertake a res-

The DSRV *Avalon* being lowered onto the after deck of the British Polaris missile submarine *Repulse* in preparation for a simulated rescue mission. The *Avalon* was flown across the Atlantic to the Firth of Clyde, Scotland, in a demonstration of the DSRV's mobility. The craft are designed to mate with standard submarine hatches, thus providing a universal rescue capability. (U.S. Navy)

The rescue submersible *Avalon* rests on the after deck of the British Polaris submarine *Repulse* during the April-May 1979 exercises of the U.S. undersea craft with Royal Navy submarines (U.S. Navy)

cue from a stricken submarine. Their capability was demonstrated in several exercises, being flown to another port from their San Diego base and then taken to sea by submarine. These exercises employed several U.S. submarines in the supporting "mother" role as well as one British submarine, HMS *Repulse*, in 1979.

The even more ambitious DSSV deep-ocean search and recovery vehicle was not built, for the reasons that led to a reduced DSRV program. The DSSV would have been about the same size as the rescue craft, but with a single pressure sphere to accommodate two operators and two relief operators, with an endurance of 30 hours at three knots. The DSSV would also have been transportable by air and submarine, and fitted with devices to locate and pick up small objects, such as weapons and satellite components, from depths to 20,000 feet.

One other vehicle was developed under the nominal aegis of the Deep Submergence Systems Project, the nuclear-propelled NR-1. This vehicle was conceived by Admiral Rickover to test a small reactor in the deep-ocean environment and provide a long-endurance research and work vehicle. Although begun in Admiral Rickover's nuclear propulsion office within the Navy, overall management was shifted to the deep submergence organization because of its extensive work on submersible systems and operations.

The NR-1 was constructed at Electric Boat, being completed in 1969. Details of the craft are difficult to obtain, although when built it was announced that the craft would be made available for civilian operations as well as military missions. But the latter operations have predominated for the NR-1. The craft has a submerged displacement of 400 tons, is 136½ feet long, and has a submarine-like appearance. Inside are accommodations for a five-man Navy crew plus two scientists. Power is provided by a small pressurized-water reactor, with two propellers and tunnel thrusters providing a high degree of maneuverability. Special features include sonar for navigating and locating seafloor objects, and a large recovery device. In 1976 the NR-1 helped to recover an F-14 fighter that rolled off the deck of an aircraft carrier, coming to rest in 1,960 feet of water. Published reports indicate that the NR-1's operating depth is about 3,000 feet.

Admiral Rickover had proposed building a series of submersibles like the NR-1, but much higher than announced costs, and the general decline of interest in deep-ocean activities have resulted in the NR-1 being a one-of-a-kind—albeit remarkable—craft. (Admiral Rickover formally proposed an NR-2 in 1976, but lack of Congressional and Navy support resulted in no funds being made available. Subsequently the craft was designated HTV for Hull Test Vehicle, to emphasize its use of improved steel to serve as a research craft for advanced combat submarine materials. Delays have continued, with construction of the HTV tentatively planned for the late 1980s.)

The U.S. Navy continues to operate deep submergence vehicles in scientific and military roles, both as adjuncts to military submarine activities and to support other Navy and national programs.

The *Halibut* approaching San Francisco's Golden Gate bridge with a deep submergence vehicle on board. (U.S. Navy)

The NR-1 comes alongside a pier at the New London submarine base with the help of a tug. Note the craft's low sail structure, small sail-mounted diving planes, and fixed mast. Special underwater search-recovery equipment is mounted on her deck. (U.S. Navy, Jean Russell)

The NR-1 at sea with the television camera mounted atop her fixed, stub mast taken out by a censor. The craft does not have conventional periscopes or any weapons capability. However, she has been used to recover weapons as well as other material from the ocean floor, and to support the Navy's seafloor acoustic monitoring systems. (General Dynamics/Electric Boat)

Appendix B
SUBMARINE-LAUNCHED BALLISTIC MISSILES

The following table provides characteristics of the four ballistic missiles carried by U.S. submarines from 1960 onward. The design of U.S. SLBM submarines have permitted the forty-one craft initially built to carry the Polaris to be modified to carry successively improved versions of the Polaris. The later thirty-one submarines could also be modified to carry the Poseidon. Subsequently, the last twelve submarines were modified to carry the Trident C-4 missile.

The new *Ohio* (SSBN-726) class of submarines will initially carry the Trident C-4. The Trident D-5 missile will be carried only by the *Ohio* class.

The missile names are secondary designations, with a letter-number designation indicating the missile sequence. Missing designations (e.g., C-1) are designs that were not developed or not produced.

TABLE 12. SUBMARINE-LAUNCHED BALLISTIC MISSILES

Missile	Polaris A–1	Polaris A–2	Polaris A–3	Poseidon C–3	Trident I C–4	Trident II D–5
Operational	Nov. 15, 1960–1965	June 26, 1962–1974	Sep. 28, 1964–1981	Mar. 31, 1971–	Oct. 20, 1979–	1989 est.
Weight (pounds)	30,000	30,000	36,000	65,000	65,000	~126,000[4]
Length (feet)	28½	31	32⅓	34	34	44
Diameter (inches)	54	54	54	74	74	83
Powered Stages	2	2	2	2	3	3
Propellant	solid	solid	solid	solid	solid	solid
Range (n. miles)	1,200	1,500	2,500	~2,000–2,500[2]	~4,000	~6,000
Warhead	nuclear 1 RV ~1 MT	nuclear 1 RV ~1 MT	nuclear 3 MRV[1] 200w KT each	nuclear 8–14 MIRV[3] 40 KT each	nuclear 8 MIRV 100n KT each	nuclear MIRV

1. Multiple Re-entry Vehicle.
2. Varies with warhead loading.
3. Multiple Independently targeted Re-entry Vehicle.
4. Preliminary characteristics.

INDEX